# OVERCOMING JEALOUSY

**A Publication of the Applied Ethics Research Group**
(Groupe de recherche en éthique appliquée - GREA)

**Other Works Published by GREA in the Same Series:**

*Shifting Perspectives:
Changing Your Outlook for Positive Results
(Changer de regard)*
By Olivier de Brivezac and Emmanuel Comte
Translated by Benjamin Ivry

*The Ethics of Minor Actions (L'Éthique des Petits Actes)*
By Eric Camerlynck
Translated by Benjamin Ivry

# OVERCOMING JEALOUSY

By Béatrice Guernier and Agnès Rousseau

Translated by Benjamin Ivry

PARAVIEW
Bracey, Virginia

Copyright © Nour Foundation, 2006

All rights reserved, including the right to reproduce this book or portions thereof in any form whatsoever. For information, address Paraview, Inc., 40 Florence Circle, Bracey, VA 23919.

ISBN: 0-9764986-4-2

Library of Congress Cataloging-in-Publication Data

Guernier, Beatrice, 1956-
 [Vaincre la jalousie. English]
 Overcoming jealousy / by Beatrice Guernier and Agnes Rousseau ; translated by Benjamin Ivry. -- 1st Paraview, Inc. ed.
    p. cm. -- (GREA series)
 Includes bibliographical references.
 ISBN 0-9764986-4-2 (alk. paper)
 1. Jealousy. I. Rousseau, Agnes. II. Title.
 BF575.J4G8413 2006
 152.4'8--dc22
                           2006025251

First Paraview, Inc. edition 2006

Manufactured in the United States of America

## Acknowledgments

The authors would like to thank all those who made this work possible by candidly answering questions, sharing their experiences, and participating in the introspective exercises and analyses set forth in this book.

# Contents

**Acknowledgments** v
**Preface** ix

**Jealousy Defined** 1
The Source of Jealousy 3
Varying Degrees of Jealousy 9
    Gradations in Intensity 9
    Gradations in Extent 11
    Gradations in Manifestation 14
The Scope of Jealousy 17
    Whom Do We Envy? 17
    What Do We Envy? 22

**From Effects to Symptoms** 25
Psychological Effects 27
Behavioral Effects 33
Mental Effects 41
Spiritual Effects 43

**Therapy** 51
Thinking Differently 53
    Creating Motivation 54
    Autosuggestion 59
Behaving Differently 67
    Driving Away Jealousy 67
    Abstention: Struggling against Malevolence 67
    Taking Action: Practicing Benevolence 68
Some Prerequisites for Success 75
    Detecting and Recognizing our own Jealousy 75

| | |
|---|---|
| Perseverance | 78 |
| Spiritual Intention | 79 |
| An Immediate Remedy | 80 |
| Methods for Detecting Jealousy | 83 |
| Starting with a Common Symptom of Illness | 83 |
| Making an Interim Diagnosis | 84 |
| Making a Definitive Diagnosis | 85 |
| A Practical Plan for Overcoming Jealousy | 87 |
| Suggested Exercises and Analysis | 88 |
| **Summary** | 91 |
| **Conclusion** | 97 |
| **For Further Reading** | 99 |

# Preface

The titles published in the *Daily Ethics Collection* recapitulate lectures presented in the framework of a seminar organized by the *Fondation Ostad Elahi: Ethique et Solidarité Humaine*[1] (The Ostad Elahi Foundation: Ethics and Human Solidarity). Focusing on ethical attributes and their application in daily life, the lectures offer valuable insight into the subject at hand and grapple with its concrete and practical variations in different situations and contexts. Written in an engaging style made livelier and more accessible by the plentiful inclusion of anecdotes, the ensuing studies favor a realistic and pragmatic approach principally aimed at encouraging and illuminating an ethical process etched in the heart of daily experience.

Each book in this series offers reflections on an ethical (or unethical) attribute, familiarizing us with its various manifestations, causes, and effects, as well as methods for further developing or counteracting the attribute under study. In each case, the goal is to grasp how certain aspects of daily behavior that have become so customary as to seem innate often impede our progress, thus acting as an invisible barrier that blocks the development of our humanity.

---

1. www.fondationostadelahi.fr; see also www.ostadelahi.com

The authors who founded the *Groupe de recherche en éthique appliquée* or *GREA* (The Applied Ethics Research Group) have spent considerable time researching and investigating analyses developed by Ostad Elahi[2] that encompass mankind's spiritual dimension and originate from the source of transcendent divinity. At the same time, the theoretical component of this work has derived from a variety of diverse sources in philosophy, law, psychology, and religion. The explanations and concrete examples presented here are the results of the group members' personal research and experiences.

---

2. Ostad Elahi (1895-1974) was a philosopher, musician, and jurist whose realm of thought in the field of ethics greatly surpassed the boundaries of his profession, making him a wise and sacred personality of the 20th century. His innovative and modern philosophy of perfection addresses some of the major questions that have been raised about mankind's origin, identity, and eternal destiny.

# JEALOUSY DEFINED

If we set aside the issue of amorous jealousy for a moment, jealousy signifies the negative emotion we feel when we see another person benefiting from an advantage that we do not have, or would like to be the only one to have. That jealousy is a negative feeling cannot really be disputed: jealousy makes us bitter about another person's pleasure, causing us to secretly hope for his failure and to rejoice in his misery. What needs to be emphasized about this definition is that jealousy registers a threefold relationship: the jealous person himself; the object of his desire; and the 'other' person, the one who is envied because he possesses the object of desire. Moreover, being jealous does not just mean desiring something—it involves desiring something that we do not have but someone else does. As this emotion becomes more pronounced within us, we reach a point where we can no longer even stand the fact that another person might also possess what we have, and this matter serves as a source of constant distress for us.

Strictly speaking, the difference between jealousy and envy is often distinguishable. The envious person suffers from another person's good fortune and wants for himself what the other person has, whereas the jealous person simply fears having to share with another an advantage to which he feels exclusively entitled, or fears losing that advantage to the benefit of another.[1] Nevertheless, this distinction is not strictly observed in daily usage, and the word "jealousy" tends to be used for both instances. In addition, the word "envy" does not exist in all languages. For the sake of simplicity, therefore, we will use these two words interchangeably, noting simply that the words "jealousy" and "envy" should be understood to encompass all the various and often subtle nuances of the attribute under study.

---

1. On this subject, see the essay "Envy and Jealousy" (Envie et jalousie) in *Dictionnaire d'éthique et de philosophie morale*, edited by Monique Canto-Sperber (Paris: Presses Universitaires de France, 2001).

# The Source of Jealousy

The etymology of the word jealousy derives from the Greek word *zelos*, for ardor or zeal. As the word implies, jealousy is an urge that foments something: it arises from an attachment to materialism, from the desire for exclusive possession and the intense attraction that pulls us towards something. The jealous person wants to possess whatever he deems advantageous—whether money, power, resources, beauty, knowledge, recognition, honors, etc.—and in particular wants it for himself alone. This is the distinguishing element that sets jealousy apart from other attributes such as covetousness or greed.

In his book *Medicine of the Soul*, Dr. Bahram Elahi explains jealousy in the following manner:

> "Jealousy stems from the instinct of possession or, more precisely, envy shrouded in selfishness. The instinct of possession is a natural characteristic that is beneficial in normal doses, for it keeps us stimulated and active. If left uncontrolled, however, this instinct deteriorates into jealousy."[1]

The concept of selfishness, then, elucidates what the jealous person desires—to eliminate others in order to pos-

---

1. Bahram Elahi, *Medicine of the Soul*, p. 38 (London: Cornwall Books, 2001). Tr. Note: Professor emeritus of pediatric surgery and the author of several medical textbooks in the fields of anatomy and pediatric surgery and urology, Prof. Elahi has spent the past 40 years concurrently studying, practicing, and teaching the subject of ethics and natural spirituality based on the philosophy of his late father, Ostad Elahi.

sess the object of his desire alone. Pleasure derives not so much from the object itself, as from being the only one to have it. This matter is tied to an old story dating back to the dawn of humanity.

In the well-known Biblical story of Cain and Abel, God accepts Abel's sacrifice but rejects Cain's, causing Cain to become jealous of his brother to the point of feeling compelled to kill him. Of course, we are not all murderers, but eliminating our rivals, which is one of the main aspects of jealousy, often occurs in a variety of ways that can be more or less overt and aggressive in nature.

Among the attributes that may be transformed into jealousy is the instinct of possession, which is not inherently noxious. On the contrary, it is a natural inclination that is necessary for our development. In its natural state, this attribute takes on the guise of emulation. When we emulate someone, we engage in a form of healthy competition with that person that drives us to achieve our best; in reality, the fact that the other person has an advantage is motivational and energizing for us. Therefore, simply wanting something is not a negative attribute per se, whereas suffering because others enjoy certain advantages and wishing to deprive them of those advantages becomes a negative quality. In his analysis on envy, Aristotle noted:

> "Emulation is ... a good feeling felt by good persons, whereas envy is a bad feeling felt by bad persons. Emulation makes us take steps to secure the good things in question; envy makes us take steps to stop our neighbor from having them."[1]

---

1. Aristotle, *Rhetoric*, Book II, Ch. 11, trans. by William Rhys Roberts, (Oxford: Clarendon Press, 1924).

Another root of jealousy is vanity and conceit, the pride that causes us to want to be supreme in domains in which the possibility of appearing prominent presents itself.[1] When we see that someone else has succeeded in such a field, we suffer because—mistakenly or not—we feel discarded and belittled, and therefore inferior to others. This feeling generates negative thoughts (about our own sense of inferiority or the world's unfairness) and negative reactions (we approach others with bitterness or directly harm them). Similarly, we may also feel jealous of the admiration meted out to one of our close friends, especially if we know that the esteem is overstated. In such a case, jealousy is bolstered by a sense of injustice that not only provides a justification for being jealous, but also all kinds of excuses that make us oblivious to our own jealousy. In so doing, it convinces us that the admired person deserves less praise than we do. Behind this seemingly justified and righteous anger, however, jealousy plays a primary role.

> "I am quite a shy and withdrawn person who prefers to be alone rather than with a group of strangers. Despite this problem, I have a strong need for friends. Since it is difficult for me to talk to people I don't know, it is extremely hard to forge friendships. On numerous occasions I have felt jealous of those who manage to make friends easily. When I am with such individuals, I want to hide this feeling and never show any outward sign of jealousy. Yet within myself, I nurse a feeling of rage, asking

---

1. Another factor that often engenders jealousy within us is the attention and affection that others receive, exactly as if the amount of love they are shown is equivalent to the amount of affection withheld from us.

myself why this person should enjoy such popularity with others and not me? What usually upsets me more than anything else is my belief that such people do not deserve so much attention. What's interesting and causes me to feel jealous is their ability to speak in public and the fact that they are always surrounded by so many people. At the end of each episode, I feel a strong sense of injustice and ask myself: 'How can a relatively dim person rivet the attention of others to such an extent?'"

This feeling of injustice is the source of the most painful jealousies. In particular, for those who are more selfish, the success, popularity, and affection others enjoy are truly unbearable. As they are internally convinced that they're more deserving of such boons, they ask themselves: "Why them and not me?" So in most cases, our suffering is tied to the feeling that our self-perceived worth and merit have been slighted. We imagine that because someone possesses something, we have probably lost something.[1] Or if someone possesses something that we don't, it's because we are inferior to him, which explains the lack of self-confidence that accompanies jealousy.

The following account provides striking proof of this notion:

---

1. Along these lines, St. Thomas Aquinas has noted that "another's good is apprehended as one's own evil… when a man is sorry about another's good, in so far as it threatens to be an occasion of harm to himself, as when a man grieves for his enemy's prosperity, for fear lest he may do him some harm." "*Whether envy is a kind of sorrow?*" St. Thomas Aquinas, *Summa Theologica*, tr. by Fathers of the English Dominican Province. London: Burns, Oates, and Washburne, 1912-36; New York: Benziger, 1947-48; New York: Christian Classics, 1981); Second Part of the Second Part; Question 36; Article 1.

"Some time ago, I felt extremely jealous of my older sister. To date, I have been more successful than she has, and must admit that in my heart of hearts have always considered myself superior to her. One day in the midst of a conversation with my mother, she expressed admiration for my sister, especially for her 'modesty and the inner beauty she radiates.' While I outwardly confirmed this praise, it set off a protest within me along the lines of 'Then what about me?' The admiration I thought that I alone enjoyed abruptly slipped away. Knowing for a fact that I possessed none of the qualities which touched my mother so deeply, I was seized with self-loathing because of all the advantages I had been so proud of just a short time before."

# Varying Degrees of Jealousy

Jealousy is not a uniform emotion—it includes shades and degrees whose descriptions enable us to grasp the danger of neglecting it and to realize what a tiny twinge of jealousy can develop into if left unattended. Three sorts of gradations can be discerned in jealousy: 1) gradations of intensity in the emotion that is felt 2) gradations in its scope and extent, and 3) gradations in its various manifestations.

## Gradations in Intensity

*First level*: We only desire to have what others possess and suffer from not having it. For instance, if I have failed a test, I become upset when I see that one of my friends has successfully passed that same test. Or if I'm rather shy in social situations, I become upset when I witness someone else being praised and admired.

*Second level*: Not only do we desire to possess what others have, but we also suffer if they were to benefit from the same advantages that we have. For instance, if I pass an exam, the fact that my friend also passes that exam ruins my pleasure. Or if I'm the center of attention at a party, I become upset at anyone else who may strive to be noticed.

> "The wife of one of my friends told me that her friends dropped her the moment she got married, found a good job, and moved into an apartment. Until that time, her friends had felt sorry for her

lot in life. They helped her and even pitied her, all the while 'unconsciously' feeling superior to her. But when they started to see her as a rival, meaning when she came into possession of some of the same privileges they enjoyed, jealousy cooled their relationship with her."

**Third level**: We are ready to relinquish whatever we have or could have, provided that others do not gain access to it either. For instance, we are willing not to work with a friend and to deprive ourselves of his expertise so that we do not have to share what we know with him. We deliberately forego all our opportunities to ensure that he doesn't possibly succeed.

> "I have practiced martial arts for years. Four years ago, a new student showed up who quickly made tremendous progress. We were supposed to work out together, but I decided early on to practice by myself to prevent him from becoming better than me. I even resolved not to compete in matches for which he had signed up out of fear that he might defeat me. By exercising alone, we definitely impeded our development. Yet at the time, I felt such a need to be better than he was that I preferred to lose something rather than for him to surpass me."

The following folkloric tale demonstrates the sort of jealousy that causes us to inflict harm upon ourselves so as to prevent another from receiving some benefit:

> "One day, a prodigal King traveling through a destitute region encountered two young brothers.

They were impoverished orphans, as inseparable as two sides of the same coin, who survived as beggars. The King was in a good mood and wanted to somehow help them. He suggested that each of them make a wish that he would grant. He started with the younger brother: 'You, tell me what you'd like, and I vow that I'll grant it. Yet be aware that whatever I grant you, I shall give double to your older brother.' The younger brother thought for a moment and then, grinning widely, replied: 'Poke out one of my eyes!'"

In the story above, we can discern several manifestations of jealousy that exist in daily life on a number of social levels, including the fact that our prosperity or misery—no matter how great—is instantly diminished in intensity as soon as it becomes clear that it has to be shared with someone else. Moreover, it demonstrates how we prefer misery to prosperity, provided we're certain that our allotted misery will somehow prevent the other person's prosperity and make him equally miserable, if not more so.

## Gradations in Extent

At the first level, we are content with being jealous of the people around us and those with whom we live or interact regularly. Then we start becoming jealous of friends of friends, then friends of friends of these friends, to the point that we wind up being jealous of anyone who seems to possess anything of value at all, whether we are in contact with him or not.

> "I am deeply jealous by nature. The slightest thing can make me jealous, and worst of all I am fully aware of this. I very much want to be the wittiest, smartest, most charismatic, loved, and important person in the entire world. With this ambitious desire, I have reached a point where I am jealous of anyone who amuses people, gets too much attention, or even temporarily becomes the object of general approval. It is difficult to admit, but nonetheless true, that if I am not the center of attention for a given time, I become jealous of anyone I lay eyes on."

Finally, the time comes when we reach the point of being jealous of people whom we should not logically envy, those with whom we share common interests. For instance, it is natural for a mother or father to rejoice when their children succeed, since to a certain extent their children's success is the equivalent of their own. To envy one's own children thus constitutes a particularly advanced form of jealousy, one more common than most people would suspect.

> "I was talking to my mother-in-law who had another child, a daughter, in addition to my husband. We talked about how life used to be when she was younger, what women could and could not do, and what had changed for the better and worse. She started to talk about her daughter, who had been a brilliant student but had found it hard to simultaneously combine a career and family life. She spoke to me about these problems in a fairly captious tone ('we can't do everything together at

once'). I discerned a degree of dissatisfaction, irritation, and, perhaps worse, jealousy in what she said. I changed the subject discreetly, returning to her own life and trajectory, and continued the discussion a bit longer. She told me that her greatest regret was not having an education. She was upset at her mother, who had only been concerned with marrying her off. That comment suddenly made something clear for me in my mind, and I understood why she declined certain invitations and social contacts ('They are all highbrows, you know'). This disillusionment had given her a complex so intense that she nursed a severe resentment towards her daughter solely for having escaped her own bitterly unfair fate. Seeing her daughter enjoy the success and self-confidence that she had always desired, without having made any effort for it but simply because times had changed, made her feel sick, like a victim of her own circumstances and generation."

Along the same lines, we might also mention the jealousy some people feel towards their spouses:

"I met my husband at college, where we shared the same major. By the time I reached the final exams for my degree, I was pregnant. I had to stop my studies and get a job, whereas he continued his coursework and obtained his doctorate as well. After a few years of teaching, he landed a prestigious and upwardly mobile job in the publishing industry. As for me, I continued as a substitute teacher in a variety of schools in the suburbs of Paris. While speaking to a female friend about my marital problems, I realized that a latent jealousy has always existed between us: I envy his professional success and connections, while he expresses his jealousy of me by cunningly opposing everything I might do to advance in my profession, as if he wants to be the only one to succeed."

Based on the accounts above, we can better gauge the extent to which the feeling of jealousy can be harmful, how it can act against our own best interests, and how it can even extend to those who are dearest to us and for whom we otherwise feel admiration and love.

## Gradations in Manifestation

*First level*: We are jealous, but we do not allow our feelings to show, and we are even willing to do anything to keep them hidden from others. For instance, if I learn that my friend has passed an exam that I have previously failed on four occasions, I try to smile and outwardly rejoice, going as far as to warmly congratulate him … even if his success upsets me inwardly!

*Second level*: We allow our jealousy to show, but not too much. We do not initiate the first step, but nor do we deprive ourselves of the pleasure of participating in minor attacks against the person we envy. For instance, if someone bad-mouths the classmate of mine who passed the exam that I had failed, I don't mind if the person continues to disparage my classmate.

*Third level*: We are overtaken by jealousy and, despite taking the initiative in carrying out an attack, still outwardly express our jealousy. For instance, I spread a rumor that my classmate passed the exam by cheating. Or, for example, I expose some of his weaknesses by saying that although he passed the exam, his behavior was scornful towards his fellow classmates. In such cases, the jealous person himself makes negative statements or carries out ill-intentioned deeds directed towards the envied person.

# The Scope of Jealousy

> *The deeds or possessions which arouse the love of reputation and honor and the desire for fame, and the various gifts of fortune, are almost all subject to envy; and particularly if we desire the thing ourselves, or think we are entitled to it, or if having it puts us a little above others, or not having it a little below them.*[1]

## Whom Do We Envy?

In order to be jealous of someone, the following conditions are necessary: 1) to be able to identify with the other person[2] and 2) to imagine that one has the right to possess what the other person has.

Jealousy is usually accompanied by the fear of not obtaining what we consider to be our just deserts. Therefore, in the first instance we are jealous of people who are situated on our own level and to whom we can readily compare ourselves. It is possible for such people to be our rivals insofar as we can be—or start to be—competitive with them.

This concept is abundantly expressed in philosophical investigations of jealousy. Aristotle stressed that jealousy targets our equals and peers, those who are "equals in birth, relationship, age, disposition, distinction, or wealth."[3] In

---

1. Aristotle, *Rhetoric*, Book Two, Chapter X, Article 4, translated by W. Rhys Roberts (Rhetorica in W.D. Ross (ed.), *The Works of Aristotle Translated into English* (Oxford: Clarendon Press, 1924).

2. Psychoanalysts call this mental identification: I could have been in the place of the person I am jealous of, who has occupied my place. On this subject, see Denise Lachaud, "Jalousies" (Paris: Denoël, 1998).

3. Aristotle, *Rhetoric*, Book II, Chapter X, Article 2, translated by W. Rhys Roberts (Rhetorica in W.D. Ross (ed.), *The Works of Aristotle Translated into English* (Oxford: Clarendon Press, 1924).

addition, it is directed at those who are near to us in time and place: "We do not compete with men who lived a hundred centuries ago, or those not yet born, or the dead, or those who dwell near the Pillars of Hercules."[1]

Along the same lines, Spinoza noted that a person can only envy "his equal, who is assumed to have the same nature as himself."[2] This jealousy can begin quite early, as the following recollection by a female schoolteacher affirms:

> "At the end of a recess period, I learned that Virgile, one of my students in CE2,[3] had pulled down the pants of his friend Nathan, who is also in my class. When I found out about this, Virgile at first denied that it had ever happened. Finally he admitted doing so, since several of his classmates had witnessed it. Virgile explained, 'I didn't do it on purpose. I was just mad at Nathan.' As I was working with my students on sensitivity training about ethical thinking, I seized the opportunity to form a roundtable discussion with the class, using this incident as a case for discussion. The students in the group went over the circumstances and asked Virgile some questions. After a while, they tried to trace the source of his anger. Aline, one of the girls in the discussion group, described a scene she had witnessed prior

---

1. Aristotle, *Rhetoric*, Book II, Chapter X, Article 5, translated by W. Rhys Roberts (Rhetorica in W.D. Ross (ed.), *The Works of Aristotle Translated into English* (Oxford: Clarendon Press, 1924).

2. Benedict de Spinoza, *Ethics*, Tr. by Robert Harvey Monro Elwes, (London: G. Bell & Son, 1883), Part III, On the Origin and Nature of the Emotions, Prop. LV.

3. Tr. note: CE2 (Cours élementaire 2) is a grade of the French primary school system in which students are usually eight years old; it is equivalent to the third grade of the American primary school system.

to this incident: 'While Nathan was playing with Sophie, Virgile came over and said, 'Oh, they must be in love!" Aline added, 'I wonder if Virgile was a little jealous? Sophie and Nathan certainly do get along extremely well.' Virgile replied, 'I don't know. I wasn't jealous, but Nathan forgets all about me when he plays with her. I asked him if he wanted to play and he didn't even answer, he just ignored me. So at some point it finally got on my nerves.'"

The history of science is also replete with anecdotes in which noted scientists are plainly envied by their fellow colleagues. The attacks which led to the final verdict against Galileo in 1633 actually started years earlier. In 1610, Galileo published *The Starry Messenger,* a work which would spread his fame and reputation throughout Europe; it would also be accompanied by a noticeable change in his material circumstances. He was appointed to a professorial chair at the University of Florence, which increased his income without requiring him to teach. Around this time, one of Galileo's friends warned him against the predictable results of this success:

> "The power and generosity of your Prince allows us to hope that he will acknowledge your merit and devotion. Yet in the stormy seas of royal courts, who can be certain to avoid—if not being shipwrecked—at least being storm-tossed by the raging squalls of jealousy?"[1]

Thus, although the attacks against Galileo apparently originated with the church, they were orchestrated by pro-

---

1. As cited in Jean-Pierre Maury, *Galilée: Le messager des étoiles* (Paris: Gallimard, collection "Découvertes," 1986).

fessors who felt their authority and power threatened by his discoveries.[1]

Jealousy, then, often develops among people who find themselves in a competitive relationship, even if it is hypothetical or imaginary, as in the following account:

> "Once, I found myself really disliking another woman. Everything about her irritated me, from her clothes to her opinions to her manner of speaking. In fact, you could say that I hated her. On the other hand, she had quite an endearing husband who had excellent qualities that inspired my admiration, to say the least. In reality, however, there was a huge gap between his intellectual and social attainments—his qualities and skills—and my own. One day I realized that I was terribly jealous of this woman. I felt as if she were my rival, even though the whole situation was entirely on an imaginary level."

As stated above, we may feel just as jealous towards an enemy as we do towards someone whom we like and admire. Surveys and experiences reveal that we are more readily jealous of those who are close to us rather than people whom we barely know, or with whom we have less in common. In reality, we are more likely to share similar values with people close to us, and it is enough to simply

---

1. On this subject, see Jerry Bergman, "The Galileo Myth and the Facts of History," *Creation Research Society Quarterly*, 39 (4), March 2003, pp. 226-235. The author argues that most of Galileo's problems derived from protests from his scientific colleagues, who were jealous of the favored treatment he received from the Church and the Duke of Florence. Further, the Church was dragged into the controversy primarily by pressure from the academic community.

have a common interest and to know about other people's lives and their history of success to increase severalfold the likelihood of being jealous.

The simple fact of loving or appreciating someone, therefore, is not enough to inoculate us against jealousy.

> "I have realized that I can feel jealous of people whom I care for deeply, and who resemble me most in terms of personality and social status. I have a female friend who was a classmate of mine for several years before we both failed our entrance examinations to graduate school at the same time. After much thought, I ultimately decided to study for the Third Cycle.[1] Feeling content about my somewhat novel idea and relief at finding a way to continue my academic studies, I relayed this plan to my friend, who was as lost as I had been in terms of her future study plans and was thus delighted by my idea. When I saw her a few weeks later, I realized she was trying to obtain the same Third Cycle diploma that I was pursuing—this upset me to no end. I was deeply disturbed that she would try to do the same thing that I was doing. After pondering the matter for some time, I realized that my emotion was a form of jealousy, for I had wanted to monopolize the situation for myself."

---

1. Tr. note: In the French educational system, graduate students who plan to focus on research will register for the 3eme cycle to obtain a diplôme d'études approfondies (DEA), a two-year diploma which is the first stage of preparation for a doctorate.

## What Do We Envy?

What incites our jealousy more than anything else is seeing someone possess, or have the possibility of possessing, what we ourselves or society consider as valuable. For instance, if we become upset when we see our neighbor's new car, it's because of the value we attribute to owning a fine automobile or the image and social standing of owning one. In the film *Amadeus* directed by Milos Forman, although Salieri is jealous of Mozart's musical genius, he says the following about the young prodigy: "He was my idol."[1] Or in the case of Galileo, because his detractors were well aware of the value of his scientific discoveries and the fact that they could not debate or attack him on scientific grounds, they shifted the debate onto religious grounds.

We might not believe that we have a jealous nature because the conditions for the expression of this emotion have yet to converge within us. For example, we may be associating with people who have nothing that we consider worth envying. Or, on the contrary, we might be socializing with people who enjoy benefits to which we cannot even begin to aspire. All that is needed to activate our jealousy, however, is to come into contact with someone who possesses what we desire or what we believe we deserve most in this world.

---

1. Tr. note: The Italian composer Antonio Salieri (1750–1825) is described in Peter Shaffer's play *Amadeus* (1979) and the 1984 film based upon it as envying his professional rival, the musical genius Mozart.

## Spiritual Jealousy

JEALOUSY INVOLVES EVERY DOMAIN, even religion and spirituality. In these fields, we can find the same mechanisms at work as elsewhere: the desire to attain something, circumstances of rivalry and need, as well as the fear of loss and being overlooked or ignored. The only difference is that in the case of spiritual jealousy, the object of our jealousy is divine attention, specific gifts, talents, powers, honors, spiritual rewards, or even divine assistance (that is, who God helps the most).

Religious history is full of incidents in which people envy someone for having what they see as a special spiritual aptitude or a sign of being close to God or His envoys. Along these lines we can cite the biblical story of Joseph, in which he relays to his brothers how he saw himself above them in a dream, thus unwittingly stoking jealousies already created by their father's favoritism:

"Now Israel loved Joseph more than all his children, because he was the son of his old age: and he made him a coat of many colors.

And when his brethren saw that their father loved him more than all his brethren, they hated him, and could not speak peaceably unto him.

And Joseph dreamed a dream, and he told it his brethren: and they hated him yet the more.

And he said unto them, Hear, I pray you, this dream which I have dreamed: For, behold, we were binding sheaves in the field, and, lo, my sheaf arose, and also stood upright; and, behold, your sheaves stood round about, and made obeisance to my sheaf.

> And his brethren said to him, Shalt thou indeed reign over us? Or shalt thou indeed have dominion over us? And they hated him yet the more for his dreams, and for his words.
>
> And he dreamed yet another dream, and told it his brethren, and said, Behold, I have dreamed a dream more; and, behold, the sun and the moon and the eleven stars made obeisance to me.
>
> And he told it to his father, and to his brethren: and his father rebuked him, and said unto him, What is this dream that thou hast dreamed? Shall I and thy mother and thy brethren indeed come to bow down ourselves to thee to the earth?
>
> And his brethren envied him; but his father observed the saying."[1]

Although we know that we are jealous, it is not easy for us to accept it. This is true for all weaknesses, but even more so for jealousy. It is one of those shameful emotions we all try to conceal from other people and ourselves, for it is indicative of a feeling of inferiority and miserliness whose existence no one likes to acknowledge within himself. Sometimes the object of our jealousy can be vague, such that we can't put our finger on it; at other times, we may also have a feeling of superiority to—or worse yet, disdain for—the envied person, a feeling that conceals from us the cause of our heedlessness, which is none other than our jealousy. In order to detect our jealousy, therefore, we must begin by identifying its symptoms and effects within us.

---

1. Genesis 37, 3-11; *The Holy Bible*, King James Version (New York: American Bible Society, 1999).

# FROM EFFECTS TO SYMPTOMS

In this section, our intention is not to offer a complete index of symptoms and effects, but rather to provide our own personal experiences and those that were shared with us. To elucidate the subject, we have divided the effects of jealousy into four main categories:

- Psychological effects: What are the consequences of jealousy on the psychological state or temperament of an envious person?

- Behavioral effects: How can certain kinds of behavior be definitive signs of jealousy?

- Mental effects: What are the effects of jealousy on the thoughts of a jealous person, as well as on the thoughts of the person who is the object of jealousy?

- Spiritual effects: What are the effects of jealousy on our relationship with the divine Source?

# Psychological Effects

One of my female friends lived near a group of very dear friends of mine. Because of family and professional developments, I had to move to a different area. Although I tried everything to prevent this move, it became imperative all the same. Each time that I met my friend, she told me about our mutual friends, their get-togethers, and the fun they had—all sorts of experiences in which I would have liked to participate. I saw clearly that she meant no harm in telling me all of this. Nothing about her behavior or what she said was intended to upset me, yet my heart still felt like it was being wrung. She expressed her affection for me by telling me secrets, which I should have recognized as proof of her friendship. Yet negative feelings burgeoned within me each time she spoke of such matters. It was some time before I finally realized that I was jealous. At first, I was convinced that my negative feelings towards her were justified. I told myself that I should distrust her since she was obviously tactless and determined to distress me. Since I felt so bad, I finally began to disparage certain aspects of her personality. I would tell myself, 'She is truly obtuse to talk to me in this way. I hope I don't ever become like her, or do this kind of thing to anyone else.'"

As the above experience demonstrates, a jealous person's envious feelings often backfire and the person primarily harms himself, which is why the philosopher Spinoza classed this emotion as one of the "sad passions"[1] that inherently weaken and depress us by reducing our physical and psychological dynamism.

In general, the manifestation of jealousy in our psyche is coupled with a feeling of sadness, melancholy, and unhappiness regarding the prosperity of others, especially those who are close to us.

> "My husband and I decided to put off having children. We preferred to place a priority on our professional lives, and I personally never wanted children. When my younger sister (who is four years my junior) informed the whole family that she was pregnant, I felt slightly depressed instead of rejoicing like everyone else. This emotion lasted until the following evening. For a certain time, I concluded that despite my claims to the contrary, I surely must have a frustrated desire to have children, and my feeling must be a form of jealousy towards my sister. After the baby was born, I realized that it did not interest me any more than babies usually did, and I noticed in particular that it represented quite a heavy burden for my sister, whose health is delicate. I was jealous less of her having a child than the status accorded to pregnancy in our family circle. Everyone takes care of you, and you temporarily become someone of importance."

---

[1]. Tr. note: In "The Ethics," the Dutch philosopher Baruch (Benedictus de) Spinoza (1632-1677) wrote: "Envy is hatred insofar as it affects a man so that he is sad at the good fortune of another person and is glad when any evil happens to him." B. de Spinoza, *Ethics*, def. XXIII at the end of Part 111, in *The Chief Works of Benedict Spinoza*, tr. R.H.M. Elwes (New York: Dover, 1955), p. 178.

Yet most of the time, we do not fathom the main reason for our sadness and are amazed by our own reactions. We want to be alone, to curl up by ourselves without realizing that this condition could be related to a latent jealousy. When we feel depressed without any apparent reason, it may therefore be useful to ask: "Why am I sad? When exactly did I begin to feel this way?" If this feeling began when we observed the joy or success of another person—or merely suspected as much—it is a sign that we are jealous. Not being happy about the joy of others, or to even feel sad in response, is thus an extremely important indicator to which we should pay attention.

It is interesting to note that from the time the first effect of jealousy appears within us—not feeling happiness for the joy of others—we gradually begin to rejoice at their misfortune as well.[1] This feeling is often expressed in an understated manner, which makes it hard to identify the symptom. Consequently, a profound self-analysis is sometimes needed to perceive this feeling internally. There is a gradation between a rough and ready response such as "I'm glad that happened to him!" and this barely noticeable state, a feeling which keeps us from truly empathizing with others and sharing their grief. In such cases, our display of empathy is merely superficial, for in our hearts we are actually quite happy about their misfortune.

> "Among my colleagues, I come into contact with a man who is far more active and intelligent than I.

---

1. Along the same lines, we are often upset when a person of whom we are jealous is praised, and are pleased when he or she is spoken ill of or criticized. Though we are often quick to believe any slanderous remarks that go around on the subject, we need years to change our negative views as a result of the things that we hear.

He has a great capacity for work and a real gift for expressing himself verbally, even off the cuff, all of which makes me quite jealous. One day his wife told me that he had to have emergency surgery due to a sudden cardiac arrest. Even as I empathized with her, I was not internally certain of my sincerity. I did not dare admit it to myself, but after trying to be honest I realized that I felt a certain pleasure at knowing that her husband was temporarily laid low. Although I struggled mightily within myself to banish this feeling, it still exists!"

When jealousy is severe, the guilty feeling described in the anecdote above turns into an acute pain, which often begins with the feeling that our heart is being wrung. We can thus understand why Ostad Elahi has stated that jealousy is like an acid that "first attacks its beholder...."[1] The psychological suffering that jealousy engenders within us is like a burning sensation that eats away at our hearts. This acid can ruin our thinking and ultimately turn into a complex. In such cases, we develop a morbid curiosity about the people whom we envy. This curiosity is almost masochistic, since it usually only augments our own suffering. Thus a woman might examine with morbid curiosity the slightest details of an outfit worn by a woman who is prettier than she, or a man might closely track the income of a brother-in-law who is imbued with financial success. In the film *Amadeus*, Salieri goes as far as paying someone to spy on what Mozart does at home, so he can know what music Mozart is thinking of and how he composes it.

This manner of behavior may sometimes assume a quite discreet, even contradictory guise. Thus, at a dinner

---

1. Ostad Elahi, *100 Maxims of Guidance* (Paris: Robert Laffont, 2000).

gathering, a mixture of foreboding and indifference, interest and disdain can lead us to listen in on conversations and extract news that will reassure our jealousy about the person whom we envy: "So, he didn't succeed in getting back together with so and so, hasn't found a job yet, and is still waiting to publish his book ... what a shame; that's the way life is!" Without daring to admit that we are dying to relieve our jealousy, we allow ourselves to hunt down the most dubious details. This kind of unavowed curiosity is one of the most subtle and perverse expressions of jealousy. Indeed, a jealous person actually nourishes his jealousy by seeking assurance that there is basically no reason to be jealous.

Here as well, we observe that we can proceed from effect to symptom. If we perceive that we are too inquisitive about the joys and woes of other people, or too concerned about one specific person, then we have to acknowledge the possibility that jealousy may be at the root of our impulses.[1]

What makes a jealous person's predicament even worse and more complicated is that the rapid progression of his jealousy soon causes it to overflow and reach the object of his envy. The full text of Ostad Elahi's maxim aptly refers to this point: "The acid of jealousy first attacks its beholder and then permeates its surroundings."[2]

---

1. Conversely, if we are excessively distant and unconcerned about what happens to other people or to a specific individual, this may derive from self-inhibiting behavior we have adopted to suppress one particular manifestation of jealousy—curiosity—which has not managed to modify our feelings of jealousy profoundly.

2. Ostad Elahi, *100 Maxims of Guidance* (Paris: Robert Laffont, 2000)

# Behavioral Effects

In behavioral terms, the external manifestation of jealousy may start with a cool and distant attitude towards someone, as the following account describes:

> "The year I took my bac exam,[1] my best friend became close with another classmate. News of this was gradually absorbed by our circle over the course of the year, but I kept my distance from this new girl without really knowing why. Whenever she joined in one of our conservations, I would immediately fall silent. If she came over and sat next to me, I would promptly pretend that I had to go and speak to someone else. If she asked a question, I would answer it curtly, and I kept a straight face at her jokes. Sometimes, if I discovered that she was going to be at one of our parties, I would suddenly remember that I had to stay home and finish an assignment. When I analyzed this situation in retrospect, I observed a true state of jealousy within myself. Although she did everything on her part to try and please me, I continued to discreetly ignore her. I felt genuine pleasure in being the only one among our friends whom she did not manage to get close to. In truth, I believe I wanted to prevent her from totally integrating into our circle."

In the case above, as well as in those which follow, jealousy becomes all the more difficult to discern as it is

---

1. In the French educational system, the baccalauréat exam (the bac), a comprehensive standardized test, is taken at the end of lycée (secondary school).

coupled with a feeling of superiority over the envied person. This feeling of superiority helps to mask our symptoms, for how can we possibly envy someone whom we perceive as inferior? The answer is quite simple: in a vague way, we perceive the person as a threat and think that he might compromise our privileges (for example, by gaining access to special individuals or being praised by others for his specific talents). We can detect an element of jealousy in this threatened feeling, as we strive to preserve our exclusive enjoyment of some benefit, status, reputation, etc.

More openly hostile behavior can ensue after this initial coolness, in which case we become a selfish individual who views the envied person with disdain and strives to highlight his weaknesses. In social settings, we systematically opt to turn discussions to subjects with which he is unfamiliar. We take a dig at him or relish evoking his failures in order to belittle him and tarnish his good name. For instance, if someone seeks to praise the remarkable way in which he has balanced his career and family life, we try to diminish the value of what he's done by saying: "Of course, he's really fortunate that his parents are always around to take care of the children," or, "I'm not convinced that his marriage is really that ideal … you know, appearances can often be deceiving."

> "My wife pointed out that I was exaggerating when criticizing the performance of a colleague whose work I don't find satisfactory. I replied that I wasn't criticizing him, and at any rate there was no reason for me to be angry at him—the whole subject wasn't worth the trouble.' I even tried to temper my disdain with a kind of false empathy along the lines of 'even if his work isn't that great, deep down he's

really a nice guy....' Despite all this, my wife's comment gave me some doubts. When I thought about the situation at length, I realized that I am upset with this person, for he enjoys a good relationship with someone whose friendship I seek. Since that time, I have felt a little hurt or angry whenever anything good has happened to this colleague; in fact, just hearing him or his work praised by someone is enough to irk me, which leads me to conclude that my critical stance towards him must be a form of resentment or jealousy."

In the account above, resentment led to the person belittling and disparaging anything that his colleague attempted to do or any success that he achieved. The belittlement and systematic criticism, however, are mere stopgaps that only serve to temporarily relieve our suffering, ultimately leaving behind a bitter aftertaste. In this kind of example, the problem is that we cannot perceive our jealousy when it first manifests. All the signs lead us to think that we have no reason to be jealous of such a person, since we don't really consider him worthy. After all, why ever should we envy Mr. or Mrs. So-and-so, who is merely an insignificant person? Under these circumstances, the symptom of the illness, which normally serves to reveal it, actually works to mask the illness.[1] Among the other expressions of jealousy, we can also note pretentiousness (which in a sense is another means of belittling the opposing person).

---

1. These examples illustrate a mechanism whose functioning Spinoza has aptly defined: if we imagine that someone owns a thing which we love, and he relishes it with a comparable or closer connection than that which we would have had we possessed it alone, our feelings may transform into hate or contempt towards the loved thing itself (*Ethics*, III, 35). Thus we are moved to belittle what in reality we desire. Spinoza points out: "This

> "I realized that when I'm with a friend whom I do not compete with directly, I tend to stress some of my talents, qualities, projects, successes, and personal accomplishments; in short, I show off unobtrusively. I have also observed that occasionally I mention with subtlety the important things that I do (things the other person does not do), and the fact that I'm entrusted with this or that responsibility. It took me some time to discern this fairly discreet form of pretentiousness; upon further reflection, however, it became abundantly clear that such behavior derives from my jealousy."

In the example cited above, showing off is used as a stopgap strategy. By inciting us to be pretentious and to affirm external signs of dominance in order to humble the opposing person, showing off makes us temporarily forget that we feel threatened by the envied person.

Jealousy impels us to seek and find the slightest faults of the person whom we envy while refusing to acknowledge his good qualities, negatively interpreting his achievements, and magnifying our misjudgments about him. The French author Jean Toulemonde considered that this sudden acumen for pointing out other people's failings constitutes one of the major effects of jealousy:

> "Our attention is focused on the slightest defect and prevents us from seeing—or admitting the existence of—any positive qualities. A jealous woman

---

hatred towards an object of love joined with envy is called Jealousy, which accordingly is nothing else but a wavering of the disposition arising from combined love and hatred, accompanied by the idea of some rival who is envied." (*Ethics*, III, prop. 35, Note). This odd blend of love and hatred, admiration and disdain, makes jealousy exceedingly hard to grasp.

will not concede that a rival is lovely, even when her beauty is unquestionable. Yet she will immediately detect the first sign of crow's feet etched into her rival's face and readily point out her fashion faux pas. An author whose books are not selling well will deny the value of a fellow writer's works, lingering over imaginary stylistic oversights and feverishly thumbing through the text in the hopes of discovering an error or a case of incorrect usage."[1]

Ultimately, jealousy can lead us to harm those whom we envy: this can take the form of slander, libel, withholding of information, or throwing monkey wrenches of every kind into the works—there are many ways in which we can violate other people's rights. Jealousy nourishes within us the active part of our psyche that is ever ready for doing harm and transgressing the rights of others, a part which Prof. Elahi has aptly termed the "imperious self."[2] The imperious self leads us to adopt aggressive behaviors aimed at destroying others. This destruction can be directed towards the individual himself (as when Mozart was destroyed by Salieri in *Amadeus*), his social status (as when Galileo was sentenced to house arrest and banned from communicating with other scientists), or his fame. In the latter case, the example of Marie Curie, who after receiving her second

---

1. Jean Toulemonde, *Les Inquiets* (Paris, Payot, Collection "Petite Bibliothèque Payot" 2002) p. 261. Tr. note: The original edition of Jean Toulemonde's study, *Worriers*, (so far untranslated into English) is as follows: Jean Toulemonde, *Les Inquiets: Caractériologie - thérapeutique* (Paris: Payot, 1953). Jean Toulemonde was a specialist in Natural Sciences who taught at the Faculté Libre des Lettres et Sciences Humaines of Lille, France.

2. For a more detailed explanation, see Bahram Elahi, M.D., *The Path of Perfection* (Virginia: Paraview, 2005), Chapter Six.

Nobel Prize was accused by journalists of carrying on a love affair with Paul Langevin,[1] is highly indicative of behavior that can be induced by jealousy. In his book *Zadig*, Voltaire describes well some of the excesses of jealousy.[2] One jealous character in particular presents all the symptoms of an emotion that even affects his features, and leads him to unjustly accuse Zadig of a crime. If Voltaire's descriptions seem caricatured, their exaggerations have the virtue of making them easier to analyze:

> "Facing his house was the home of Arimaze, a character whose wicked soul was depicted on his gross physiognomy. He was ridden with malice and swollen with pride, and worst of all, he was a tedious wit. Never having managed to shine in society, he took his revenge by maligning it. Despite his wealth, he found it difficult to assemble flatterers at his home. He was annoyed by the sound of carriages entering his courtyard in the evening. The sound of someone singing his praises irked him even more. Sometimes he would visit Zadig's house uninvited and sit down to dinner; he would compromise the entire pleasure of the company, as it is said that Harpies contaminate the meats which

---

1. Tr. note: The Warsaw-born French scientist Marie Sklodowska Curie (1867-1934). With her husband Pierre Curie (1859-1906), she was awarded half of the Nobel Prize for Physics in 1903; in 1911 she received a second Nobel Prize, this time in Chemistry, in recognition of her work in radioactivity. After her husband died, Curie had a love affair with Langevin, who was married at the time.

2. Tr. note: In his philosophical tale *Zadig* (1747) set in ancient Babylon, Voltaire (1694-1778) discusses the problem of evil. In the story, Zadig is a young man who suffers from the jealousy of others, being jailed repeatedly without reason.

they touch.[1] One day he decided to extend a party invitation to a lady, who instead of accepting, went to supper at Zadig's home. Another day, while they were chatting in the palace, they ran into a Minister who invited Zadig to supper, while pointedly not inviting Arimaze. The most unrelenting loathing is often based on nothing more significant than this. The man, who was called 'the envious one' in Babylon, wanted to get rid of Zadig, because he was known as 'the fortunate one.'"

In terms of symptoms, we certainly cannot assert that coolness, slander, and generally harming others are definitive signs of jealousy. In the same way that fever is not always symptomatic of flu, violating the rights of others may be a sign of an ethical weakness, such as a voracious ambition or an overdeveloped spirit of vengeance. Nonetheless, if we discover such behaviors within ourselves, it cannot hurt to engage in some self-analysis to discern the real source of these feelings. One reliable way to gauge if jealousy is actually at work is to analyze how we feel when confronted by the success or failure of the person in question. Thus, we might seek a pathognomonic indicator,[2] which in the case of jealousy is easily detectable: suffering from another person's happiness and rejoicing in his misfortune.

---

1. Tr. note: In Greek mythology, the mythological creatures Harpies, winged monsters, are sent to Phineas, a king of Thrace, to contaminate his food.
2. Tr. note: A pathognomonic indicator is a medical term referring to a specific symptom for an illness or disease, which is all that is often required for a diagnosis.

# Mental Effects

Like any other negative emotion, jealousy emits an energy to which others do not remain indifferent. Even if they are unaware of its nature, people receive the energy emanating from us and, like a boomerang, send it right back. Jealousy results in making us unpleasant to others and causing them to treat us coldly and, on occasion, aggressively. In terms of symptoms, let us assume that X is on good terms with Y, and this relationship suddenly cools. X would be spontaneously inclined to say that the problem is Y's, or, even worse, that Y is jealous of him. Yet the opposite theory can also be true: Y may be intercepting X's jealousy, and unconsciously keeping his distance because he is unknowingly trying to protect himself from X.

> "I got along very well with a female friend of mine. After she got married, we continued to see each other for some time. Her husband was then promoted to quite a high level in his company, with a proportionate raise in his salary; that is when I sensed a split between us. I felt that she looked down on me and I was no longer good enough for her. Gradually we stopped seeing each other. Later, after talking to someone else, I realized that her attitude stemmed from my own jealousy. She grew apart from me because she observed that I envied her and she could no longer allow herself to act naturally with me. What confirmed my intuition was that when I began resisting this envious feeling within me, her attitude towards me changed."

One of the effects of jealousy, or indeed of any feeling that derives from the imperious self, is that it creates a field of negative energy around the jealous person, like an acidic smokescreen that harms anyone who approaches it. Consequently, when our jealousy persists, others clearly begin to depreciate us and may at times even be inclined to shun us.

# Spiritual Effects

## Jealousy Corrodes the Substance of our Soul

The emotion of jealousy creates a sudden rebellion from the negative energy flowing within us that serves to undermine our spiritual health. If this energy is not opposed by positive energy, it results in not just making us more jealous, but also intensifying some of our other weaknesses; depending on the seriousness of our illness, it may even denature some of our virtues. For instance, if we do not internally struggle against our jealousy, there is a strong likelihood that slander and ungratefulness will also burgeon within us, or we may simply become malevolent and transgress the rights of others. As a result of the progression of this disease, our spiritual substance gradually becomes corroded, exactly as if they were constantly pouring sulfuric acid on us and destroying all of our tissues and organs.

## Jealousy Obstructs our Understanding of Ourselves and Others

> "Jealousy notices everything, except what really exists."
> —Xavier Forneret[1]

If acquired virtues are like lit candles within us that illuminate our beings and flood us with light,[2] then jealousy, like every other weakness, creates a point of darkness within

---

1. Tr. note: Xavier Forneret (1809-1884) was a French poet, playwright, and journalist.
2. Bahram Elahi, *Medicine of the Soul* (London: Cornwall Books, 2001), p.52.

us that obstructs the light and thus prevents knowledge of ourselves and others. Rooted in obliviousness to our own condition, virtues, and real needs, our jealousy ultimately exacerbates this lack of awareness and further darkens our field of perception. In so doing, it leads us to not only see others negatively—meaning to misjudge their intentions and merits—but also to close our eyes to ourselves; in short, we deceive ourselves through our jealousy. For instance, when other people upset us, we are quick to blame and malign them at the first opportunity, often without even being aware that our feelings stem from our jealousy.

> "In our office, one of my female co-workers who is my age outranks me because she has two years more seniority. Yet, because of my professional qualifications, as soon as I was hired our boss assigned some projects to me that were previously her responsibility. She gave every sign of taking this fairly well. For one thing, it meant less of a workload, which she had been requesting for some time from management. For three years now we have been working together. Sometimes we squabble, but mostly we get along, even though we are not close. Once, three months ago, I became seriously upset at her behavior. She came over and advised me about a matter concerning my private life, without my having requested anything of the kind. She suggested that given our current workload, I should reduce my fairly hectic social life. I did not reply, but for the rest of the week I nursed negative feelings towards her. I told myself that we could not get along, which was normal, since our personalities were too dissimilar. I constructed an entire theory about the fact that some people are impossible to get along

with, and there is no need to investigate why. I confided in a psychologist friend, who amazed me by suggesting that I might try asking myself whether I envy her. I explained to him why I felt that this could not be the case. Yet from that moment on, I strove to detect any signs of jealousy within me. I must say that since then, my friend's suspicions have been partially confirmed."

## Jealousy Anchors Spiritual Ungratefulness

In spiritual terms, if we believe in divine mercy we see that jealousy places us in a position of ungratefulness; in other words, we no longer acknowledge or appreciate the graces that have been bestowed upon us by the divine Source. We are jealous because we believe we deserve more than the person whom we envy. In reality, this amounts to telling God, "Why didn't you give that to me?" By which we are implying, "I deserve that too," or, even worse, "I am the only one who deserves it," or ultimately, "I deserve it more than the other person." Believing that we are more deserving sparks a feeling of unfairness within us, which may be expressed through rancor towards God. Thus, we no longer accept that He is just and benevolent, and gives us everything that we deserve and more still. If we allow a minor, latent ungratefulness to take hold within us, it can ultimately lead to a rebellion against God. In Milos Forman's film *Amadeus*, Salieri feels that he deserves the gift of musical inspiration more than Mozart, and eventually rebels against God. Forman expresses this rebellion through the blasphemous symbolic image of burning a crucifix. Without reaching such an extent or being quite as explicit, it is clear that burgeoning ungratefulness, sulky rejection of

God, and a sense of unfairness—all of which nourish jealous feelings within us—are factors that decrease our spiritual motivation and faith. Along these lines, we can cite the Gospel story of the Prodigal Son:[1]

> "And he said, A certain man had two sons:
> And the younger of them said to his father, Father, give me the portion of goods that falleth to me. And he divided unto them his living.
> And not many days after the younger son gathered all together, and took his journey into a far country, and there wasted his substance with riotous living.
> And when he had spent all, there arose a mighty famine in that land; and he began to be in want.
> And he went and joined himself to a citizen of that country; and he sent him into his fields to feed swine.
> And he would fain have filled his belly with the husks that the swine did eat: and no man gave unto him.
> And when he came to himself, he said, How many hired servants of my father's have bread enough and to spare, and I perish with hunger!
> I will arise and go to my father, and will say unto him, Father, I have sinned against heaven, and before thee,
> And am no more worthy to be called thy son: make me as one of thy hired servants.
> And he arose, and came to his father. But when he was yet a great way off, his father saw him, and had compassion, and ran, and fell on his neck, and kissed him.

---

1. The Gospel According to Saint Luke, Chapter 15: 11-32, *The Holy Bible*, King James Version (New York: American Bible Society: 1999).

And the son said unto him, Father, I have sinned against heaven, and in thy sight, and am no more worthy to be called thy son.

But the father said to his servants, Bring forth the best robe, and put it on him; and put a ring on his hand, and shoes on his feet:

And bring hither the fatted calf, and kill it; and let us eat, and be merry:

For this my son was dead, and is alive again; he was lost, and is found. And they began to be merry.

Now his elder son was in the field: and as he came and drew nigh to the house, he heard musick and dancing.

And he called one of the servants, and asked what these things meant.

And he said unto him, Thy brother is come; and thy father hath killed the fatted calf, because he hath received him safe and sound.

And he was angry, and would not go in: therefore came his father out, and intreated him.

And he answering said to his father, Lo, these many years do I serve thee, neither transgressed I at any time thy commandment: and yet thou never gavest me a kid, that I might make merry with my friends: but as soon as this thy son was come, which hath devoured thy living with harlots, thou hast killed for him the fatted calf.

And he said unto him, Son, thou art ever with me, and all that I have is thine.

It was meet that we should make merry, and be glad: for this thy brother was dead, and is alive again; and was lost, and is found."

Many of the subjects we have discussed about jealousy are found in the parable above.[1] In terms of its spiritual effects, if we consider the father to represent God, we can clearly see how the older brother—who nurses a feeling of unfairness because he considers himself to be the more spiritually deserving son—progressed from envying his brother (who was so close to him) to feeling anger against his father (God). The older brother's jealousy led him to resent his father and to forget or be blind to all the goodness and gifts his father had always lavished upon him ("Son, thou art ever with me, and all that I have is thine."). What is interesting is that by refusing to join the celebration, he deprives himself of divine grace and mercy, which is symbolized here by the feast. Therefore, the feeling of rebellion that stems from jealousy generally weakens our relationship with God and prevents us from aligning our wavelength with His.

As our analysis of the detrimental effects of jealousy draws to a close, we can cite the following conclusions:

---

1. We can see how jealousy often assumes the noble, righteous guise of a sense of unfairness. This feeling is genuine, yet unfounded, since of the two brothers, the jealous one is the more pampered and has less to complain about. The parable also indicates that the jealous person never really desires what the other person possesses per se, but only wants it because the other possesses it. This is evidenced by the fact that during all the years he spent laboring in the fields, the older brother never expressed the wish to sacrifice a calf in order to carouse with his friends. Therefore the Prodigal Son's return does not reveal any hidden frustration, any buried or suppressed desire. Quite simply, it causes an entirely new craving, which relates less to what his brother is given—the fatted calf and celebration—than to the preferential treatment that it may represent. The older brother covets it for himself too, and says so unambiguously: "and yet thou never gavest me a kid, that I might make merry with my friends."

➢ The jealousy that leads us to harm others will harm ourselves more than anyone else. Saint Cyprian of Carthage described the throes of jealousy as such: "Whoever of you are envious and malignant, you are seen as you are, crafty, pernicious, and hostile to those whom you hate. You are the enemy of no one's well-being more than of your own. Whoever he is whom you persecute with jealousy, will be able to escape and avoid you. You cannot escape yourself. Wherever you are, your adversary is with you; the enemy is always in your heart; destruction is shut up within; you are tied and bound with an inescapable chain of links; you are captive with jealousy as your master; and no solaces come to your relief."[1]

➢ In order to change for the better, we have to start by examining ourselves to determine what we need to alter. It is beneficial, then, to look at ourselves impartially, just as a doctor would examine a patient's body. Although we sometimes wish to eliminate all of the weaknesses within us, it is far more difficult to accept even a single one of these weaknesses when they are triggered on a specific occasion. Thus it may not be so difficult in theory to accept that we are jealous, yet if a friend were to tell us that the reason we looked glum at a celebratory dinner party for a colleague was that we were jealous of that colleague, it would be much harder to accept. It is not enough, therefore, to be implicitly aware that we are jealous; rather, we must also know whom and what we are jealous of, as well

---

1. Tr. note: St. Cyprian of Carthage, *On Jealousy And Envy (De Zelo et Livore)*, Chapter 9, tr. anonymous; The Fathers of the Church Series, Patristic Series, vol. 36. (Washington, D.C.: The Catholic University of America Press, 2000). St. Cyprian (d. 258), a third century bishop of Carthage, wrote a number of Latin treatises.

as the extent to which we are jealous and the circumstances that trigger our jealousy.

# THERAPY

# Thinking Differently

When we examine the detrimental psychological and spiritual effects of jealousy, as well as the relational problems and widespread discomfort it causes, it becomes clear that it is essential to focus on a method or strategy for effectively combating this attribute.

At the first stage, this struggle will resemble the treatment for poisoning, and at the second stage a hygienic practice for spiritual life. But we shouldn't delude ourselves: without effort and perseverance, we cannot eradicate a weakness of this kind overnight. As long as we retain the "instinct of possession"—in other words, as long as we are alive—the possibility of an excess or deficiency in the functioning of this instinct remains. Therefore, jealousy will always potentially exist or recur within us. Nevertheless, to fight against it we can utilize internal defensive reflexes so that when an onslaught of jealousy occurs, we can be aware of its presence and prevent it from becoming rooted within us.

This methodical struggle against a weak point begins—like any other work in the field of ethics—by working on our thoughts, a work based on understanding the mechanism behind the functioning of a weak point. This mental effort will then translate into action, provided that it is accompanied by a transformation in our spiritual substance. Accordingly, even if Montaigne was correct when he wrote that more than any other mental illness jealousy demands greater energy, though few are the medicines that will remedy it,[1] we

---

1. *The Essays of Michael Lord of Montaigne*, tr. John Florio. World's Classics (London: Frowde, 1904). Book III, Chapter V: "Upon Some Verses Of Virgil."

intend to show that there are in fact specific methods that are effective for treating jealousy, provided that we truly decide and commit to using our willpower, acumen, and perseverance to engage in the struggle.

## Creating Motivation

As soon as the symptoms of jealousy have been discerned, the challenge is to find the motivation within that will enable us to eliminate this weakness, or at least lessen its harmful aspects.

### *Recalling the Harmful Effects of Jealousy*

"No unjust man ever looked more like an oppressed one than the jealous man. He sees the favors which you enjoy as a punishment for himself." (Statement by a Bedouin, as reported by Abu Hamid Al-Ghazali)[1]

The first argument we can use, then, is that jealousy is unproductive and does not benefit the jealous person:

> "During my final year of lycée, I found myself in the same class as my best friend. Since the Third Class, I had been class delegate, a post which he himself had assumed since he was in the Fourth Class.[2] That year we ran against each other in the student elections. At the time, I was sure that I would win. I had

---

1. Tr. note: Abu Hamid Al-Ghazali (1058-1111 CE), a 12th century Persian-born Sunni Muslim philosopher and theologian, was the prolific and influential author of such works as *The Incoherence of the Philosophers* and *The Revival of the Religious Sciences*.

2. Tr. note: In the French educational system, the lycée is comparable to an American high school; students in the final year of lycée are usually eighteen years old. In Collège (comparable to junior high school), students in the Third Class (Troisième) are usually 14 years old; those in

been a good delegate, appreciated by my friends for my skill in defending them during dealings with the school administration. Yet he ultimately wound up winning. At first, I was so displeased I was barely able to congratulate him. Then I began making excuses: I blamed the class for choosing the wrong delegate and for preferring the 'cool' delegate to the serious one. I was extremely upset with my friend, as I had been relegated to the lowly status of substitute delegate because of him. This envy persisted until the following day. Gradually I realized that my rage and jealousy were not helping me in any way, and that I simply had to accept the facts; I had no other choice. This was hard to do, however, because it required admitting that my friends had preferred him to me. It is never easy to accept that sometimes one of our friends may be better than we are, especially for someone like me."

We must yield to the obvious and realize that to envy what others possess does not allow us to acquire those benefits. According to the musical legend, Salieri murdered Mozart, but that did not make him a Mozart. An excellent method for self-motivation, then, is to remind ourselves that this feeling is vain at best and harmful at worst. We can tell ourselves that jealousy not only adds a bitter taste to our own successes, but also stifles every joy at its origin, for when we are under the influence of jealousy we suffer because we do not possess what others have, or we're angry that others also possesses what we have. Even if we are

---

the Fourth Class (Quatrième) are usually 13 years old. In French lycées, the Class Delegate (le délégué de classe) is elected by the students as their representative in meetings with the school's director and other matters.

certain that the person we envy will not succeed in life and derive some comfort from this knowledge, the resulting happiness provided by this certainty is tinged with a feeling of sadness.

The second argument we can use is to tell ourselves that this state of mind will halt our material and spiritual development, for as long as we are under the influence of jealousy our energy is wasted on destructive and futile activities. Therefore, conceiving and nursing dark, hateful thoughts and seeking to harm others have no benefit for us.

> "For some time now, I have been in competition with a co-worker who is almost the same age and shares the same educational accomplishments. Since this began, I have mulled over bad thoughts about him and negatively interpreted everything he says or does. Instead of minding my own business and focusing on what I need to get done, I'm preoccupied with his success. For instance, even when I have mountains of files to resolve, I waste scads of time spying on him to find out what he's working on and how he approaches it. Lately, I have also observed that my relationship with him has been severed. While not giving in to slandering him, I have developed a certain coolness towards him that has caused him to avoid me. Previously we had enjoyed a rather cordial relationship, but now we rarely speak to each other and there is even a certain level of discomfort when we meet face-to-face."

It should be noted that in the experience above the harmful effects caused by jealousy depend on the nature of the jealousy involved. When we envy someone for material reasons, for example, its negative repercussions impact our material lives, meaning that we encounter some material harm or difficulty, such as the loss of a friendship or our zest for life, a professional opportunity, or some other material advantage. On the other hand, when we are envious of someone spiritually, its negative repercussions impact our spiritual lives. In this regard, one of the gravest effects of jealousy is the stunting of our spiritual progress, which is well illustrated in the biblical story of Cain and Abel. Cain envied his brother because Abel's offering was accepted by God. Imagining that he would attain his goal of attracting God's satisfaction by killing Abel, Cain actually ends up depriving himself of this very goal through his murderous act.

> "I have observed how vital it is for me to sustain a relationship with God through direct communication with Him and by confiding my feelings in Him. This is either done through prayer at set times during the day, much like a rendezvous planned in advance, or through more spontaneous impetuses. Although I am plainly aware of the tremendous benefits I derive from this relationship, lately I have felt less of a desire to have such heart to heart talks with him. I told myself that this intimacy had become second nature to me, and it was no longer necessary to dedicate as much time to my 'conversations.' This went on for a few weeks until I realized that I was deceiving myself. As I am always seeking to be cognizant of my behavior, I realized that my lack of motivation coincided with the awakening and progression of a feeling of jealousy toward someone whom I had recently come to know. Without daring to admit it to myself, I thought that this person had been indulged by God with spiritual aptitudes—especially

his grasp of spiritual matters and his level of advancement in spiritual practice in terms of fighting against his weaknesses—which I believed were preferable to my own aptitudes. Contrary to what I had thought, the reason I was communicating less with God was because I was unknowingly blaming Him for paying so much attention to this person; in short, I sulked away from Him. Because of my jealousy, for which I considered Him responsible, I neglected God and distanced myself from Him."

### *Being Cognizant of the Advantages of Not Being Jealous*

The flip side of the discussion above provides us with another source of motivation: namely, becoming cognizant of the sense of buoyancy and relief that are derived by overcoming our jealousy. Rather than being a source of resentment and despair, other people become a source of joy and delight, for a bit of every success we rejoice in becomes our own success.

Imagine a Salieri who became Mozart's friend and reached a level where he thanked God for letting him hear His voice through Mozart's music, a Salieri who would have done everything to promote Mozart's performances, thereby serving his colleague as well as all those who would have enjoyed his music. In so doing, Salieri would have done himself a good turn as well, since he would have won the friendship of Mozart, whose brilliant genius would then have reflected upon him for posterity.

### *Taking into Account the Baseness of this Weakness*

It is much easier to combat a weakness we loathe than a trait to which we've become accustomed. Learning to detest a weakness is not easy, but it's extremely effective in getting us motivated. In order to do so, we should recall all of the destructive blows we have delivered to those whom we envy. It is also beneficial to confront the hideousness of the feelings we experience when we're envious, to smell the rank odor of our malevolent thoughts, and to look carefully at the despicableness of our base thoughts. Of course, this would first require that we be aware of our weaknesses and learn how to observe our feelings and thoughts. Before we reach such a stage, however, we can help ourselves by looking into the mirrors represented by others, for it is always easier to spot a weakness in others than it is in ourselves. Therefore to see the baseness of jealousy, we can begin by observing it in others. Naturally, the purpose of this exercise is not to criticize others or to simply stop at this point, but rather to pass through the mirrors of others on our way to returning to ourselves.

## Autosuggestion

We can clearly see that more than anything else, working on jealousy is a matter of autosuggestion.[1] It is a matter of convincing ourselves internally by fighting against the justifications and excuses of the imperious self. We have tested a few forms of this autosuggestion, but it should go without saying that there are as many varieties of autosuggestion as there are types of people and jealousy.

### *Concentrating on What We Ourselves Have*

Rather than focusing our attention and energy on others, we should try to concentrate on ourselves, on what we possess

---

1. Tr. note: The French psychologist Emile Coué (1857-1926), known as the Father of Applied Conditioning, wrote widely on autosuggestion.

and others probably lack, including our material possessions, talents, quality of life (our free time, parents, spouse, children, living environment), and ethical qualities.

> "For a while I was fairly depressed and glum, and felt somewhat empty ... until one day I felt ashamed about feeling this way. I tried to trace the source of my sadness, and that's when I realized that I was being influenced by a number of external factors, i.e., someone who has a noteworthy moral attribute, another person who has a united family, etc.—in short, a variety of advantages that others enjoyed which seemed truly ideal to me. I discovered that my feelings of inferiority and emptiness were a form of jealousy and ingratitude about my own lot in life. So I decided to shift my focus from others onto myself. At first I didn't see much, but the more I continued doing this, the more I began to see, until I became certain that everything that happens to me has some meaning. This approach had many positive results, including feeling turned off by envying what others had that I didn't. For the first time, I realized that such behavior constituted a form of snooping into the private lives of others. When I saw all the graces in my own life, I realized that I'd never had the time to understand the extent to which I've always been immersed in blessings, and that enviously glaring at the lives of others had been a form of filching on my part."

Naturally, in order to reach the above conclusion, we must first enjoy a minimal degree of success. We have to be able to ask ourselves: "Am I really ready to change places with someone else?" A heavy dose of self-delusion lies at the heart of every jealousy, as we imagine that others have better opportunities or occupy better positions than we do, especially since we often do not see their difficulties and tribulations. We imagine that others are more fortunate than we are, without even knowing what it feels like to actually have the things they do. Or we imagine that an opportunity that we are pushing ourselves toward will make us prosperous, whereas that may not necessarily be the case.

> "One of my friends experienced a sudden boost in his social status, as a result of which I regularly saw him mentioned in the newspapers and even on television. Each time the opportunity arose, I always slipped in a mention that I knew him quite well; sometimes I almost made it seem as if the source of his success could be attributed to me. At first I thought that I would impress others by doing so, but then I realized that these pretentious displays—attracting the attention that was lavished on my friend and sharing in the honors he was given, which I envied—were in fact a totally false way of portraying a form of superiority over him. One day, this friend called me: he needed to talk because he felt all mixed up. He told me that his life had become arduous and that he loathed all the media exposure he was subjected to. He couldn't tolerate the constraining and treacherous effects celebrity had on his personal relationships and didn't know how to deal with the problem. Listening to him, I realized that there are two sides to every coin. I learned that my friend is rather reserved by nature and appreciates the simple pleasures of life, and that I'd had such a false impression of the joys that such

potential honors would bring me. I became convinced that I would be far better off never having to deal with such honors."

## Reflecting on Values

Another aspect of working on our thoughts is to question ourselves about the value of that which we envy. Perhaps by developing a sense of detachment, we may finally be able to allay our jealousy. This approach is especially useful in cases where we are jealous of strictly material things like money, beauty, or social success. If we are able to persuade ourselves through autosuggestion that such things are fleeting in essence, we can easily upend our jealousy as its futility becomes glaringly obvious. This mindset does not mean that we should consider what others have as worthless, but rather that we should compare only the object of our desire with other things. In any event, sometimes life's circumstances assume the task of showing us the futility of our desires:

> "One of my friends bought an expensive car. You can see how jealousy, however modest, turns people into fools. In daily life, I take no interest in cars, and they are merely a side interest. Yet on this occasion I asked myself, 'Why does he have an expensive car and I don't?' A few days later, when I managed to rid myself of these annoying thoughts, a different friend phoned me to say that I could use his car whenever I wanted, since most of the time it sat idle in a garage. It was the same make as the car belonging to the friend I had envied. Since then I often drive that car, and frankly it is quite nice. But I'm not ecstatic each time I get behind the wheel,

and in fact I often prefer to take the subway. In reality, each time that I have fought against a case of material jealousy, I have indirectly received what I wanted to have. And each time, I have discovered that the object of my envy does not bring me the pleasure which I had anticipated."

## Contemplating Fairness and Merit

As we have seen on numerous occasions, jealousy is often coupled with a feeling of unfairness. "Why him and not me," we ask. One of the ways of properly controlling jealousy, therefore, is to tell ourselves that whatever others have is the result of what they have previously merited. If someone has something that we lack, or is someone that we're not, it's because he has done something for it that we haven't. Sometimes, it might be a deed that we lacked the initiative or desire to perform. Even if we still feel that we are more deserving of something than others (since merit is often unobservable), how do we know that being in their place would be beneficial to our material and spiritual development? Moreover, if we have sincere faith in the just and compassionate creator, how could such a creator deprive us of that which we deserve, or that which is necessary and beneficial for us?

We have to grasp the reality that the envied person has not taken anything away from us, but rather is in possession of what is rightfully his. Mozart did not steal his musical gifts from Salieri, nor did Abel rob Cain of God's approval. In reality, in both cases their advantageous situation was a result of divine grace and justice. Instead of focusing on what "another person has and we don't," why not accept and admire the justice that prevents any right—whether it be ours or that of others—from being lost?

To provide an image of our situation in this world, we might compare ourselves to runners in a 200-meter race, wherein each person advances only in his own lane. Consequently, when someone wins, he hasn't taken anything away from the other competitors, since he has only focused on running in his own lane. Clearly, we cannot advance like the competitor in the lane next to us by nursing bad feelings about him; if we are to advance, we have to expend the necessary effort and energy. Therefore, instead of looking over at the runner next to us and trying to prevent him from advancing, it is better to focus on our own lane. It is also worth noting that if a runner in a 200-meter race focuses on his own task and refrains from trying to trip up the runners next to him, he will be spurred on during the race by the presence of the other competitors at his sides, which is one of the reasons why world records are seldom broken by racing alone.

> "When I started my career, my boss asked one of my co-workers to help me with a small project which I normally handled alone. Although I did not say anything so as not to make a bad impression, for a whole day I was unable to get anything done and I was tempted to simply forsake the whole thing. When I began reasoning with myself, I realized that if I continued in this manner, I would probably be fired soon, so I decided to start working. The next two months were fantastic. I would wake up at dawn, eager to be the first one to arrive at work, and I went home later than usual at nights, since we got into the habit of preparing a progress report every evening to organize our work for the following day. The environment was stimulating: the more my

rival labored, the more I was motivated to work. By observing him up close as he toiled, I had the opportunity to realize and appreciate his skill, which forged a real friendship between us."

The above observations on autosuggestion demonstrate that it is in no way a mere mechanical, repetitive, and lifeless practice. On the contrary, autosuggestion against jealousy constitutes an exercise in the field of self-knowledge and thereby a means of better knowing others and their virtues. At the same time, autosuggestion is a form of meditation and reflection on the real value of things.

# Behaving Differently

Before we are completely overtaken by jealousy, a good method for fighting against it is to drive away jealous thoughts.

## Driving Away Jealousy

To better understand the meaning of this concept, we might compare the feeling of jealousy to a mosquito. As soon as its buzzing is heard, we spontaneously wave our hands to ward it off. If we see it poised on our arm, ready to bite, we immediately react to get it away from us, sometimes killing it with our hand without the slightest hesitation. Why not treat any jealous thought that surfaces in the same way? That is, as soon as we feel a jealous thought has arisen within us, we try to drive it away with a brusque reaction of thought. This would be a way of saying no to jealousy and distancing it from us, just as we would treat any emotion whose indignities and damage we have experienced.

As we may surmise, the whole difficulty of this effort derives from the fact that we doubt the existence of the feeling of jealousy within us, for this emotion manifests in an insidious way that often makes detecting its signs quite difficult.

### *Abstention: Struggling against Malevolence*

As we have seen, jealousy makes us liable to harm those whom we envy. Therefore, the first thing to do is not to yield to the instinctive reactions that incite us to behave maliciously. For instance, if we feel like maligning a co-worker of whom we are jealous, or have the opportunity to give him wrong information, we should strive to refrain from doing so.

## Taking Action: Practicing Benevolence

What is more difficult, however, and certainly more effective is to force ourselves to do the opposite of what our jealousy impels us to do—that is, to treat those we envy with affection and benevolence.[1] In general, this "antidotal approach" is fairly effective in fighting against malevolent propensities, though it requires greater resolve to initiate and effectuate change. This approach comprises three principal axes: good will, good speech, and good deeds.

## Good Will

From the bottom of our hearts, we should strive to want good things for those whom we envy and hope that they derive the maximum benefit from their opportunities, successes, and advancement. For instance, praying for their success is an excellent exercise. Naturally, something inside of us will rebel at first: "I already envy his shameless success; now I'm to pray so that he can enjoy even greater success?"

---

1. St. Cyprian offered similar advice to those whom he sought to cure from envy and jealousy: "Love those whom you hated before; esteem those whom you envied with unjust disparagements. Imitate the good, if you can follow them; if you cannot follow them, surely rejoice with them and congratulate your betters. Make yourself a sharer with them in a united love; make yourself an associate in a fellowship of charity and in a bond of brotherhood. Your debts will be forgiven you, when you yourself shall forgive; your sacrifices will be accepted, when you shall come to God as a peace-maker." Tr. note: St. Cyprian of Carthage, *On Jealousy And Envy (De Zelo et Livore)*, Chapter 1, tr. anonymous; The Fathers of the Church Series, Patristic Series, vol. 36. (Washington, D.C.: The Catholic University of America Press, 2000).

But through steady persistence and becoming accustomed to putting ourselves in the place of others and asking, "Would I want others to be jealous of me?" and repeating to ourselves that we cannot attain God's satisfaction unless we transcend our negative tendencies, it will become easier to do so. It may take quite some time for such an effort to produce results, which is why we shouldn't forget how essential the concepts of perseverance and repetition are in this struggle.

### Good Speech

Instead of merely refraining from making negative comments about those whom we envy (stage one), we should strive to say good things about them, a slightly more difficult task. This does not imply, of course, that we should make inappropriate remarks or engage in insincere flattery, for this would merely encourage others to rectify our remarks and state things as they really are, thus causing negative things to be said about the person in question. Instead, it is better to change our outlook in such way that we truly perceive the genuinely positive qualities of the people we envy.

> "An acquaintance of mine has enjoyed tremendous success. Initially, he attained a great position in the company where I work, and later was presented with an exceptional opportunity in the new company where he now works. From the beginning, I was wary of the negative feelings I had developed towards him and I could see the imprints of jealousy behind this. Thus, I forced myself to rejoice in his success. Several extremely challenging incidents arose for me. During a lunch meeting, people who

were jealous of this same co-worker began to overtly say negative things about him. At first, I didn't say anything. Then, summoning up my courage, I sincerely tried to emphasize his positive qualities and to show his true merit. This totally changed the mood of the luncheon, not just for me—I suddenly felt a burst of positive energy—but for the others as well, as they stopped their negative remarks. Through this technique, my jealousy gradually disappeared."

## Good Deeds

In *Cinderella*, there is a scene in which the Ugly Sisters tear Cindellera's dress out of sheer envy. We can all recall scenes from kindergarten or early childhood of how one child resented another to the point of destroying his drawing or breaking his toy. For us conservative adults, who smile at such childish acts, these dramatic actions can serve as examples of the kinds of actions we are apt to commit as a result of our jealousy. As we have seen, the first step is to refrain from these sorts of rebellions. However, it would be even more effective if we were to do the exact opposite of what the imperious self is driving us to do.

> "Since graduating from school, I was aware that the professional and familial success of one of my former classmates was upsetting me deeply. I finally told myself that I am definitely jealous of him and, aware of the baseness of this feeling, decided to fight against it by demonstrating my friendship to him more openly. The opportunity quickly presented itself when a few days later he phoned to ask if I might help him move. I have to confess that

the opportunity was not exactly enticing; in fact, it was particularly arduous since we had to transport heavy sofas and furniture from one side of Picardie to the other.[1] After a brief pause for reflection, I agreed to help. I was aided in my decision by knowing that I was doing it for an ethical purpose, as I was not just trying to please a friend, but also fight my feeling of jealousy. At a time when I was gripped by envy, however, this was exactly what I had the least desire to do."

In daily life, we can seek to help the person we envy to succeed in whatever he undertakes. This help can assume many different forms, such as offering useful advice, lending our car, or babysitting for his children. But as the imperious self is quite crafty, it will intercede by raising some apparently legitimate excuses: "We shouldn't interfere in the affairs of others," "Mind your own business," "My own family's well-being comes first," and "It'll teach him a good lesson to be better organized and responsible and to stand on his own two feet." In fact, it will continue to devise so many excuses and justifications that the only thing to do is to turn a deaf ear to all such arguments.

> "One of my friends decided to take a trip with her husband. The prospect of watching her leave without her children (their grandparents had agreed to take care of them) to a place where I myself dreamed of going upset me. I thought to myself: 'Why do they have to travel so far away?' 'And is it really wise to leave such young children behind?' A

---

1. Tr. note: Picardie is a region in the north of France, comprising over 19,000 square kilometers of land.

week before her trip, my friend called me; her voice was somewhat sad. She had recently been told by her parents that they couldn't watch the children because her mother had just broken her leg. From her manner of speaking, I felt that she was hoping I would suggest something. Yet, at that time a driving force within me said, 'Let her cope with her children by herself. Besides, why does she even have two children if all she can think about is traveling? She really shouldn't abandon them like this.' At any rate, it took me a whole day of soul-searching and grappling with a guilty conscience until I offered to take care of her children. I still recall the burning sensation I felt at the time: 'I get to do this terrible task while they lie in the sun.' The thought of undertaking such an unpleasant task at the exact time she was enjoying what I myself dreamt of doing was extremely difficult for me. Despite this, I made the effort and the results were fantastic: I developed a special affection for her children, enjoyed a wonderful time during the vacation, and, in particular, the experience helped to ease the jealousy I had felt for this friend."

The main purpose of this work, which does not appear natural at first, is to dry up the source of negative energy that poisons our thinking, actions, and in general our relations with other people. As in the example of autosuggestion, this work cannot be achieved in a single attempt. In the beginning, the practice of benevolence can even increase our feeling of depression and unease, which derives from jealousy. When we begin treatment for substance abuse and are deprived of the daily dose of the drug that we had overconsumed, we feel worse than before. But with persistence and perseverance, we can be hopeful that we will ultimately regain our health.

> ### What if the Jealous Person is not to Blame?
>
> "The least that can be expected of any human being is to never make a display of his temporary superiority over others, as this can only too easily offend and wound one or another of people around him."
> —Alfred Adler[1]
>
> APPARENTLY IT IS NOT POSSIBLE to refrain from jealousy when confronted by certain remarks and behavior. Of course, it is clear that jealousy will impact ourselves and others with all of its secondary repercussions, which entail tangible psychological and emotional results. Thus it is clear that fighting jealousy is our duty, even when it is deliberately provoked in us. On the other hand, we should realize that we can also draw the detrimental effects of jealousy upon ourselves through our boastfulness, self-aggrandizement, assertion or justification of a preference, lifestyle, and mannerisms—all of which stem from a lack of

---

1. Tr. note: Alfred Adler (1870–1937) was an Austrian doctor and psychologist whose ideas, expressed in *Menschenkenntnis* (1927); *Understanding Human Nature*, tr. from the 1927 edition by Colin Brett (Oxford: Oneworld Publications, 1992), among other books, have influenced modern-day psychology. According to Adler's "Individual psychology," most people strive for "superiority," or a form of self-realization. Individuals who feel inferior react either through self-development or by seeking power, which is sparked by an inferiority complex.

self-confidence. Sometimes, even excessive enthusiasm and joy is enough to annoy or peeve someone.

Being cognizant of this mechanism encourages us to anticipate the reactions and feelings of others (after all, human nature is universal in certain respects), to encounter others with greater maturity, and to be more alert of ourselves and the circumstances present. From a humane perspective, the principles of ethics dictate that we should not draw the attention of others to that which may provoke their jealousy; conversely, a moderate approach will introduce a measure of delicacy and judiciousness into our relationships.

# Some Prerequisites for Success

To fight against our jealousy in the most effective way possible, it is necessary to observe a few conditions. Among them, we have selected three that are not just specific to fighting jealousy, but also indispensable and effective in fighting against all ethical weaknesses.

## Detecting and Recognizing our own Jealousy

There is always something that prevents us from recognizing our own jealousy. In reality, it's not easy to acknowledge that this trait lies within us. Unconsciously, we try to use all kinds of subterfuge and false arguments to convince ourselves that we aren't jealous. We tell ourselves, "Why should I be jealous of him? We don't work together in the same field, and I really think he's great." Or we might say, "I'm telling her for her own good; otherwise, nothing exists between us that would cause me to be jealous of her." In general, the best thing to do is to turn a deaf ear to all of the justifications intended to show that we're not jealous. For even if it were true that we are not jealous, what would we lose by cultivating goodwill for others?

> "For years I worked with a person who was not always easy to get along with. Except for meaningless trifles, I had no specific complaints about him. Although I did everything I could to be on friendly terms with him, internally I felt that the relationship was artificial, as if a wall of ice separated him from me. I finally concluded that our personalities were too different to be able to share a true friendship.

> As I was pondering the unease that spoiled my relationship with this co-worker, the notion that I might be jealous of him suddenly crossed my mind. At first, this was fairly difficult to admit to myself, and I was tempted to simply discard this seemingly baseless thought. After struggling with myself for some time, however, I was able to accept that I was in fact jealous of him in one respect: he was taking giant steps forward professionally in a specialized field that meant a great deal to me."

Once we admit that we are jealous, it is necessary to clearly identify this jealousy within ourselves. This can be a difficult task, for as we have seen above, this weakness often manifests in an insidious manner. The example below clearly elucidates this matter:

> "I was speaking to my supervisor's secretary about a problem that had occurred that very day. An important meeting had been cancelled because a co-worker, who was in charge of leading the meeting, forgot to attend. Thus, everyone else made the trip for nothing. The secretary told me that she would inform management about what had happened. The following day, I saw the secretary again and she told me the supervisor had laughed when he heard the story and hadn't taken it too seriously. After this discussion, I felt a little upset and depressed. I could observe my bad state, but without understanding its cause. Because I knew this feeling could be a symptom of my imperious self manifesting, I decided to delve within to try and see the situation more clearly. An inner dialogue thus began:

'Why am I upset?'
'I have no idea.'
'Since when do I feel this way?'
'Since I left the secretary's office. She was alone in the office, so this feeling must have resulted from my conversation with her.'
'What did she say that could have made me feel upset?'
'Nothing. She just relayed what our boss had said. Moreover, she was smiling and happy. I don't understand.'
'If nothing occurred apart from this conversation, then this conversation must have made me feel this way. What exactly did she say?'
'That the boss laughed and didn't take the incident seriously.'
'If that is what made me upset, it means that I would have liked him to take this matter seriously.'

Just then, as I was sincerely looking into my heart of hearts, I suddenly realized that I would have indeed liked him to take the matter seriously; I also found that I wanted the supervisor to scold my co-worker.

'Why did I want my co-worker to suffer harm?'
'I don't know.'
'Did I have any reasons for being upset at him?'
'Not a single one.'
'Might not jealousy be at the root of my ill-will?'

At that point, I recalled with bitterness the privileges he enjoyed, and thus realized that I was jealous of him. I would never have imagined it. Just to be sure, I looked for other incidents in the past in which the signs of jealousy may have been present. Indeed, I recalled a great many episodes from the past:

- ➤ I'm always aware of what he's unable to do, or what he does badly, whereas he is well-known for being highly skilled in his work.
- ➤ Recently, I spoke ill of him on several occasions, on the pretext that I had a right to do so.
- ➤ When he told me he was having problems concentrating on his work, instead of empathizing with him I felt a degree of satisfaction in my heart.
- ➤ When he told me last week that he was able to visit with someone whom we are both fond of, my heart felt like it was being wrung.

Now I have enough reasons to confirm the fact that I envy him, as I have displayed all of the symptoms."

Consequently, one of the effective ways of searching for jealousy inside of us is to irrefutably demonstrate to ourselves that we are jealous of the person in question. To do so, we need only prove that we are harboring the pathognomonic sign of this disease within us—namely, suffering from the person's happiness and rejoicing in his misery.

## Perseverance

"Only by repeatedly and persistently practicing an ethical principle will it gradually become integrated within our spiritual substance and eventually become part of our second nature."[1]

---

1. Bahram Elahi, *Medicine of the Soul*, p.36.

Jealousy cannot be dominated by forcing ourselves to be kind to someone we envy or to refrain from maligning him on just one occasion; rather, despite the obstacles that may appear, we have to repeatedly force ourselves to carry out such acts. As with any other therapy, progress in fighting against jealousy does not occur overnight—it is gradual and includes periods marked by recurrence and relapse—which is why patience and perseverance are vital qualities in terms of working on ourselves and acquiring self-knowledge.

> "I had a friend whom I was quite fond of. Yet each time she invited me to her country house, I became depressed. When I began analyzing this problem, I realized that I was jealous of her possessions. To fight this feeling, I decided to perform acts of kindness towards her. But I was shocked to find that my jealousy only doubled at the outset. Nonetheless, because I believed that benevolence was the right approach, I persisted for an entire year, ignoring my inner protests. Now I can say that every last trace of jealousy towards her has vanished, and I am even fonder of her than I was before."

As we can see, it can be dangerous to fall into despair, allow adversity to overcome us, and, worst of all, to doubt the usefulness of the benevolent approach; on the contrary, we should always keep it in mind and truly believe in it.

## Spiritual Intention

A point that often recurs in the writings of Ostad Elahi is that we cannot overcome a personal weakness without the help of divine energy. This energy provides both the motivation required for fighting our weakness and the energy necessary for its lasting, or indeed permanent, control. Without the assistance of this divine energy, we will only obtain a temporary and unbalanced result. The essential condition for attracting this energy is to act without any expectation of compensation, or more precisely with what Ostad Elahi has termed "the intention of seeking divine satisfaction." In the case of jealousy, this means that our goal in fighting against jealousy should not be to please others or to derive any sort of specific material gain, but rather to do so as a human duty. Moreover, having the intention of attracting divine satisfaction is the only way to transform our essence into the same substance as that of God's. When we say having the intention to attract divine satisfaction, it means striving to perform that which would please God.

In reality, the presence of this intention is what distinguishes hypocrisy from benevolence or "forced benevolence." Hypocrisy occurs when we feign benevolence to please others with the intention of either harming them or obtaining some material benefit, whereas internally we do not believe in benevolence and could care less about others; conversely, in the case of forced benevolence, we sincerely hope and strive to develop this quality within ourselves. Thus, we do not seek to deceive others with our intention and are instead sincere, for we are genuinely obliging ourselves to be benevolent towards others and striving to discern their good qualities in order to grow fonder of them.

## An Immediate Remedy

Ultimately, when we feel we are suddenly overwhelmed by a wave of jealousy, it is possible to counter it with a wave of divine energy. If we make a truly emotional and heartfelt plea to the divine Source, we can capture this beneficial energy, which instantly neutralizes the sinister effects of jealousy like a soothing salve. Although this approach does not constitute a long-term treatment for jealousy, it does provide a way of saving ourselves at critical moments.

> "It all happened during a seminar at college. As he often did, my professor had invited a guest lecturer (who is very dear to me) to speak to us on a variety of subjects. As we watched him speak, I suddenly felt a terrible surge of jealousy towards him. This emotion was so powerful and dominant that it was unbearable. I should add that this person is a friend of mine. I was completely panicked and couldn't control this feeling. Horrified by what I felt inside, I earnestly invoked God in the following way: 'You can see what's going on inside of me—I am suffocating with jealousy towards this person, who is my friend, and I can't do anything about it on my own. I am struggling but to no avail; I've completely lost control. Since you can see within the depths of my being, please help me to recover from this state and to remove this horrific feeling from inside of me!' It was not long after I had finished my plea that I was suddenly rid of this horrific feeling in an almost miraculous way—in an instant, my heart had become as clear as water. It was as if nothing had happened, and I was finally able to hear what was being said around me. At that point I was so overcome with gratitude that tears rolled from my eyes. It was exactly like the scenes from a play: at first I was overcome with horror, and then I suddenly felt joy. I observed this miracle occur within me, and

truly 'saw' how our terrible feelings can be taken away when we ask for His help. How powerful He is, how He consoles us, helps us, and watches over us; how truly kind and magnanimous He is."

# Methods for Detecting Jealousy

How can we realize that we are jealous of someone if we have never perceived any clear sign of this weakness towards a given person? In this section, we will present a brief and simple method for detecting this weakness within ourselves.

## Starting with a Common Symptom of Illness

A common symptom is one that is not specific to a particular disease—such as fever, fatigue, or weight loss—but does alert us to the existence of a problem. For instance, if we are feverish, we deduce that we are probably ill and should consult a physician.

The common symptoms that denote jealousy are dissatisfaction, feeling upset and distressed, and a wringing of the heart. Although these symptoms are not specific to jealousy, they help to serve as warning signs; moreover, because they are often symptoms of the manifestations of the imperious self, it is always instructive to try to discern their causes. Thus, as soon as we feel sad or worried, for example, and the cause appears vague to us, it is important to backtrack for a moment, analyze ourselves under a microscope, and search for its cause:

> 1. *Carefully examine the common symptom within us to discern its true nature*
> We should look into our hearts to determine, for instance, whether our worry and anxiety is what we suspect it to be, or whether it is a sign of discontentment instead.

**2. Conduct a precise inquiry to identify the incident that caused this symptom to manifest**

We should ask ourselves: "Since when exactly have I felt this way? Was it after a specific incident or remark? Who was responsible for it?" By doing so, we compel the imperious self to "talk" and force ourselves to find the exact incident or comment that caused this symptom to appear within us. In this way, we can prove to ourselves that the reason for our provocation was an action or remark made by a given person.

**3. Seek the true cause of the manifestation of the symptom**

As soon as we discover what's really going on, we should ask ourselves: "Why has this statement or action made me sad or upset? What was behind this statement that I really didn't like? What has been offended inside of me? What would I have preferred to happen?"

We have to find the main, hidden cause of this sadness, which requires a specific form of sincere effort. However, because the hand of the imperious self has been partially exposed (for example, we know full well that the statement made by a particular person resulted in this feeling arising within us), this effort will be made easier for us.

## Making an Interim Diagnosis

For example:

> ▷ If the reason we are upset is due to another person's possession of property, benefits, or success,

it clearly shows that we suffer from this person's good fortune, which is a symptom of jealousy.

> If the reason we are upset is due to another person having emerged from a problem or misfortune, it clearly means that we are malevolent towards him, which is another (common) symptom of jealousy.

> At this point, therefore, we can be certain that the root of these common symptoms is "alerting" us to the existence of jealousy. Now, we have to seek to prove in a conclusive and indisputable way that we are in fact jealous of the person in question.

## Making a Definitive Diagnosis

1. Search for other symptoms displayed in the past:

    > Being morbidly curious about the person in question.

    > Looking for the person's slightest flaws and refusing to acknowledge his good qualities.

    > Having a cold and distant attitude towards the person.

    > Showing openly hostile behavior towards the person, such as belittling him, making spiteful and snide remarks, recalling his failures, or ridiculing him in front of others.

    > Harming the person, engaging in slander or calumny, exploring and acquiring information related to him, sabotaging him, violating his rights, etc.

2. Look for the pathognomonic symptom

   As previously stated, the pathognomonic symptom of jealousy entails suffering from the happiness of others and rejoicing in their misfortune.

When we start with a common symptom such as sadness, distress, or depression and analyze it, we often wind up with the interim diagnosis that we are suffering from another person's happiness. Thus, all we have to do is to find an instance in the past when we rejoiced at the person's misery to conclusively establish that we are jealous of him. Identifying other examples in which we also suffered because of his happiness or rejoiced in his misery will increasingly convince us that we are indeed jealous of this person.

# A Practical Plan for Overcoming Jealousy

As soon as the therapy has been formulated, the best way to test it and engender a positive change within ourselves is to put it into practice. In the following section, a series of exercises are recommended for helping us to overcome our jealousy.

It should be noted that in such a task, each person acts as his own physician; in other words, each of us must seek the source and manifestations of this weakness within ourselves, as well as the conditions under which it appears in order to overcome it through a daily practice that requires focus and resolve.

For this exercise to be effective, we suggest keeping a log of your daily activities, similar to that which a scientist keeps to record the daily changes he observes in the subject under study, the main difference being that your experiment pertains to your own person and your own psyche. By carefully jotting down our daily observations and accurately recording our experiences and feelings, we will come to possess another useful tool for increasing our self-knowledge.

## Suggested Exercises & Analysis

Every day for at least two minutes, think about people and circumstances that have provoked, or currently provoke, your jealousy. In your daily logbook, record the names of the people whom you are jealous of, the reason(s) why you are jealous of them, and the symptoms which allowed you to identify your jealousy.

In order to detect your jealousy, you can either:

> ▹ Begin with common symptoms of jealousy you have discerned within yourself (sadness, depression, feeling upset or distressed, etc.), or

> ▹ Ask yourself the following: "Is there anyone in my surroundings whom I particularly wish to disparage or for whom I harbor negative thoughts? If the answer is yes, might there not be a feeling of jealousy behind it?

### *Autosuggestion*

*Exercise 1*

Every day for at least two minutes, focus on what you possess that others do not.

*Exercise 2*

Every day for at least two minutes, try to find the merit that led to the success of the person whom you envy.

*Exercise 3*

Every day for at least two minutes, come up with logical reasons for relativizing the value of that which you envy.

*Exercise 4*

Every day of the week, compel yourself to perform a good deed for someone whom you're jealous of. For example, do the person a favor, call him to see how he's doing, speak kindly to him, or invite him for coffee; in short, any act aimed at bringing you closer together and showing your kindness to him is a good deed.

# SUMMARY

## *Definition*

Jealousy is a negative emotion that arises within us when we see someone benefiting from an advantage that we do not have, or would like to be the only one to have.

## *Source*

"Jealousy stems from the instinct of possession or, more precisely, envy shrouded in selfishness."[1] Vanity and pride constitute another source of jealousy.

## *Scope*

What are we jealous of?
- ▷ That which we perceive as valuable.

Whom are we jealous of?
- ▷ Those with whom we are in a competitive relationship.

## *Effects*

Jealousy harms ourselves first before its repercussions afflict the person whom we envy.

- ▷ Psychological effects: a feeling of sadness (whether manifest or not) and hostility towards the good fortune and prosperity of the person we envy, as well as a feeling of satisfaction regarding his misfortune.

---

1. Bahram Elahi, *Medicine of the Soul*, op. cit.

- Behavioral effects: a cool and distant attitude towards the person we envy. In more overtly hostile behavior, we look for opportunities to humiliate or belittle the person (or to put ourselves to the fore). We seek to find the smallest weakness of the person we envy and reject his good qualities. Ultimately, jealousy can lead us to the point of harming those we envy by engaging in slander, calumny, aggressive encounters, and otherwise violating their rights.

- Mental effects: jealousy creates a field of negative energy around the jealous person, such that other people dislike him and are even inclined to shun him.

- Spiritual effects: jealousy corrodes our spiritual substance. If we do not fight against it, we will become increasingly jealous and our other character flaws will also be exacerbated, such as backbiting, ungratefulness, malevolence, and transgressing the rights of others.

> Jealousy prevents us from acquiring knowledge of ourselves and others. It makes us oblivious to our true merits and needs, and drives us to feel malevolence towards the person we envy.

> Jealousy leads us towards spiritual ungratefulness. We no longer see any of the graces we have been given, and become preoccupied solely with what the envied person possesses.

## Therapy: Thinking Differently

### Creating Motivation

In order to fight against jealousy and to persevere in this struggle, it is important to:

> ▷ *Recall the negative effects of jealousy:* the only result of jealousy is suffering, which impedes our material and spiritual progress.

> ▷ *Consider the advantages of not being jealous:* dominating our jealousy leads to our own comfort and buoyancy; the success of others becomes a source of joy for us as well.

> ▷ *Realize the loathsomeness of this weakness:* in so doing, we can come to detest it and thereby facilitate our struggle against it.

### Autosuggestion

Autosuggestion means to change our way of thinking and inwardly convince ourselves that jealousy is futile, and to gradually become aware of the true reality of all things:

> ▷ *Consider everything we have and ask:* "Am I willing to change places with the other person?"

> ▷ *Contemplate the value of things and ask:* "What is the true value of the object I covet?"

> ▷ *Reflect on fairness and merit:* By constantly reminding ourselves that God's justice is absolute and fully implemented in this world, try to eradicate the roots of the feeling of injustice within us. Ask

yourself: "How can I believe that God, who is just and benevolent, would have deprived me of something that I deserved or needed?"

## Therapy: Behaving Differently

### Acting Counter to our Jealous Thoughts

- *Driving Away Jealousy:* as soon as we become aware of our jealous thoughts, we should stop them with the force of our willpower in order to protect ourselves from their harmful effects.

- *Abstention:* we have to fight against being malevolent and wishing ill for others.

- *Taking Action:* we should act benevolently, the most effective way being to force ourselves to do the opposite of what our jealousy impels us to do.

    *Good Will:* From the bottom of our hearts, we should strive to want what is good and best for those whom we envy, and to be happy for their success. For instance, we can pray for their success.

    *Good Speech:* We should strive to see their good qualities and to speak positively of them.

    *Good Deeds:* We should do the exact opposite of whatever our jealousy impels us to do; in other words, in addition to ignoring the arguments and justifications of the imperious self, we should seek to help the person in any way that we can.

## Some Prerequisites for Success

> ➤ *Detecting and recognizing jealousy within ourselves:* the most effective way of doing so is to look for the pathognomonic symptom of jealousy inside of ourselves.

> ➤ *Perseverance:* "Only by repeatedly and persistently practicing an ethical principle will it gradually become integrated within our spiritual substance and eventually become part of our second nature."[1]

> ➤ *Spiritual intention:* Without divine help and energy, we cannot effectively fight against a weakness, for the results would be temporary and unbalanced. To receive this positive energy, we have to engage in this struggle with the intention of attracting divine satisfaction, not to derive a material gain.

> ➤ *An immediate remedy:* in critical moments, we have to invoke and take refuge in God with the utmost sincerity.

---

1. Bahram Elahi, *Medicine of the Soul*, op. cit.

# CONCLUSION

What becomes evident both from this analysis and the suggested exercises is that like any struggle in the field of ethics, fighting jealousy is not an isolated endeavor; rather, it involves many other ethical dimensions of the self. As in a system of communicating vessels,[1] it is enough to focus on a specific point and to persevere in order to engender a substantial and profound transformation of our entire personalities over time. Accordingly, working on our jealousy materially increases the quality of our self-knowledge, vigilance, and intention, as well as the benevolence in our thoughts, words, and deeds, which in turn leads to an improvement in our relations with ourselves, others, and God.

Ultimately, in our approach to this ethical work, it is recommended that we confront one by one all of the major and minor weaknesses that taint our spiritual substance, transforming layer by layer negative attributes into positive ones on a daily basis and in a continuous manner, without falling into despair, thereby becoming more humane and thus more divine and compassionate each day.

---

1. Tr. note: Communicating vessels, familiar from school physics experiments, consist of vertical tubes of different heights that are connected at the bottom by another tube. Adding or removing water to or from any one tube affects all the other tubes. In France, the notion became a literary commonplace, cf. *Communicating Vessels (Les Vases communicants)*, a 1932 study by the poet and manifesto writer André Breton (1896–1966) (tr. Mary Ann Caws and Geoffrey T. Harris; Lincoln: University of Nebraska Press, 1990).

# FOR FURTHER READING

St. Thomas Aquinas, *Summa Theologica*, tr. by Fathers of the English Dominican Province. London: Burns, Oates, and Washburne, 1912-36; New York: Benziger, 1947-48; New York: Christian Classics, 1981).

Aristotle, *Rhetoric* Book II, Chapters 10 and 11, trans. by William Rhys Roberts (Oxford: Clarendon Press, 1924).

Robert L. Barker, *The Green-eyed Marriage: Surviving Jealous Relationships* (New York: Free Press, 1987).

Jerry Bergman, "The Galileo Myth and the Facts of History," *Creation Research Society Quarterly*, 39 (4), March 2003, pp. 226-235.

Gordon Clanton, Lynn G. Smith, (eds.) *Jealousy* (Englewood Cliffs: Prentice-Hall, 1977).

Bahram Elahi, *Medicine of the Soul* (London: Cornwall Books, 2001); *The Path of Perfection* (Virginia: Paraview, 2005).

Ostad Elahi, *100 Maxims of Guidance* (Paris: Robert Laffont, 2000).

Nancy Friday, *Jealousy* (New York: Morrow, 1985).

Ayala Malach Pines, *Romantic Jealousy: Causes, Symptoms, Cures*, Second Revised Edition (London: Routledge, 1998).

Edward Podolsky, *The Jealous Child* (New York: Philosophical Library, 1954).

Peter Salovey, ed., *The Psychology of Jealousy and Envy* (New York: Guilford Press, 1991).

Peter Shaffer, *Amadeus* (London: Penguin, 1993).

Benedict de Spinoza, *Ethics*, Tr. by Robert Harvey Monro Elwes (London: G. Bell & Son, 1883).

Peter van Sommers, *Jealousy: What is it and Who Feels it?* (New York: Penguin Books, 1988).

Gregory L. White, Paul E. Mullen, *Jealousy: Theory, Research, and Clinical Strategies* (New York: The Guilford Press, 1992).

# Notes